D1370352

MANGA
COLORING

COLOR CUTE
ANIME
AND MANGA
CHARACTERS

chartwell
books

GET IN TOUCH WITH YOUR INNER CHILD AND RELIEVE STRESS BY COLORING!

Manga fans and those new to manga will love *Manga Coloring* filled with many cute and fun characters. Both anime and manga style characters are included for you to let your artistic abilities shine.

Manga is a style of Japanese comic books or graphic novels. It is written for both teenagers and adults and consists of many different genres like science fiction, romance, and fantasy. In recent years, it has become more widely known and produced in other countries outside of Japan such as Korea, China, and the United States. Japanese manga has also been translated into several languages. Now, people all over the world read and enjoy manga.

Manga Coloring includes a variety of characters from different genres. Many are also drawn in distinct styles. Some have more realistic facial and body proportions while others may have larger eyes or heads. You'll find animals, coming-of-age characters, and so much more inside.

Let your creativity flow by using bright primary colors or soothing pastels and neutrals to color in these adorable characters. Feel free to use crayons, colored pencils, markers, or even pens to fill in these pages. There are no rules, and no artistic experience is needed. The possibilities are endless!

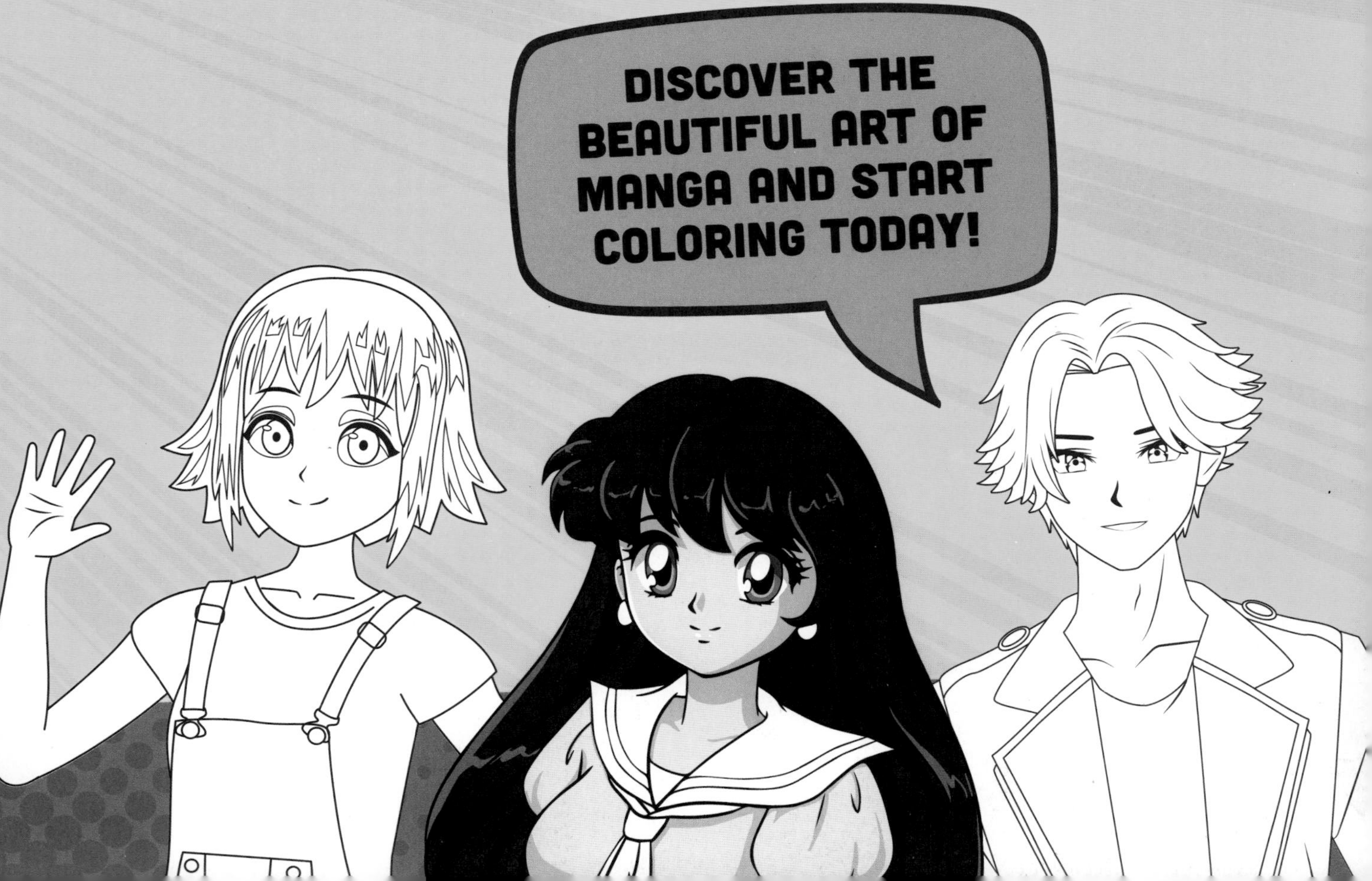
DISCOVER THE BEAUTIFUL ART OF MANGA AND START COLORING TODAY!

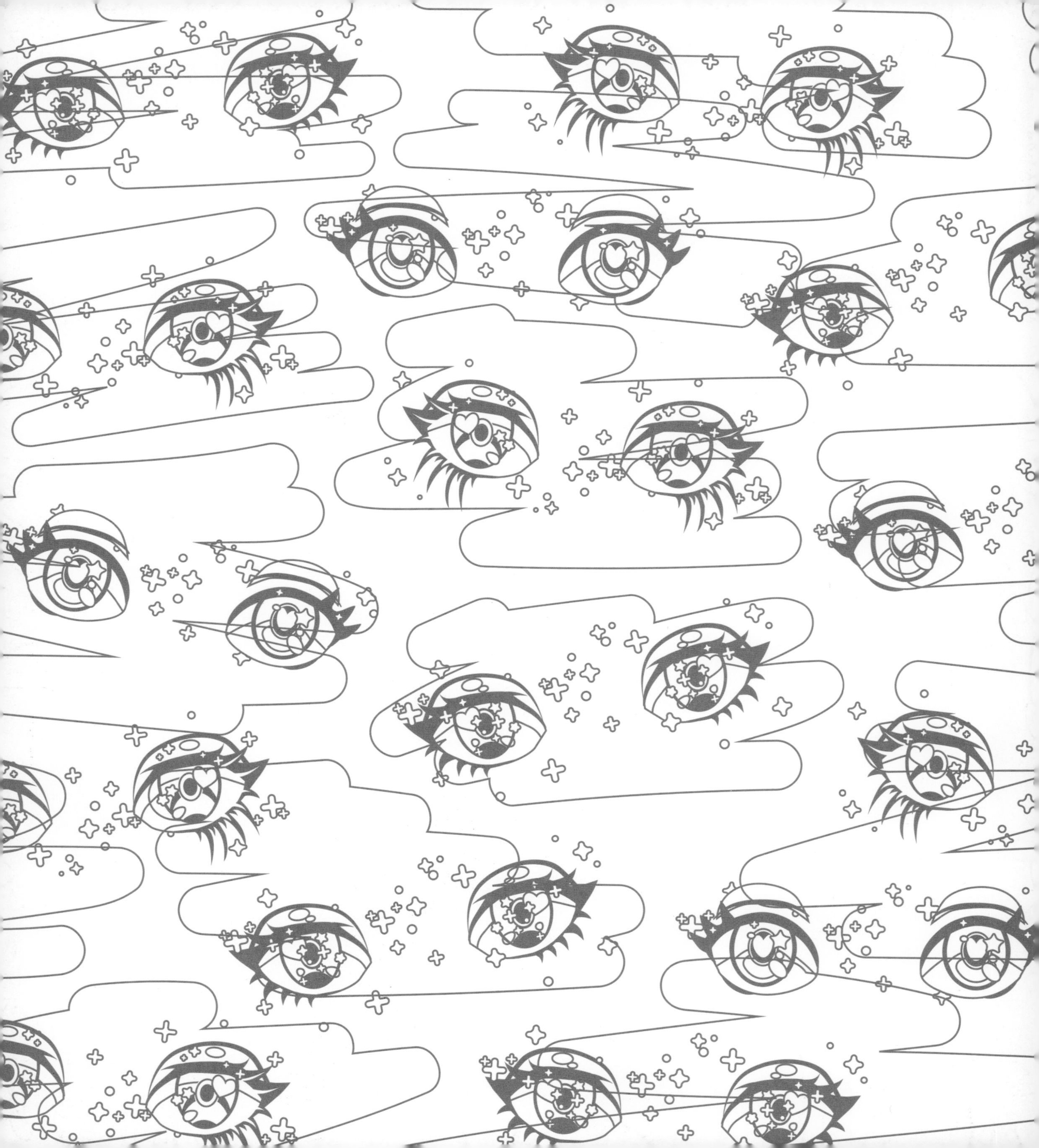

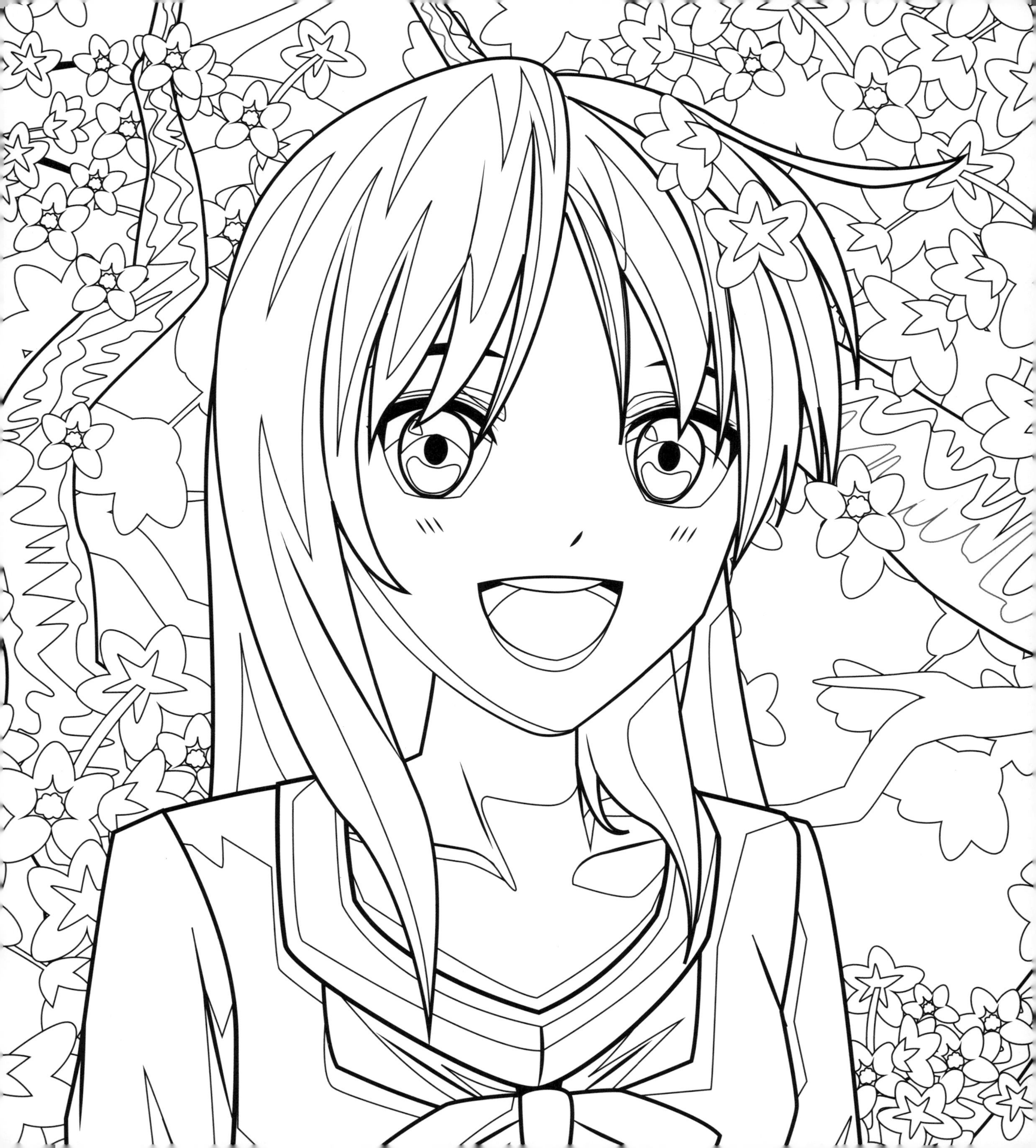

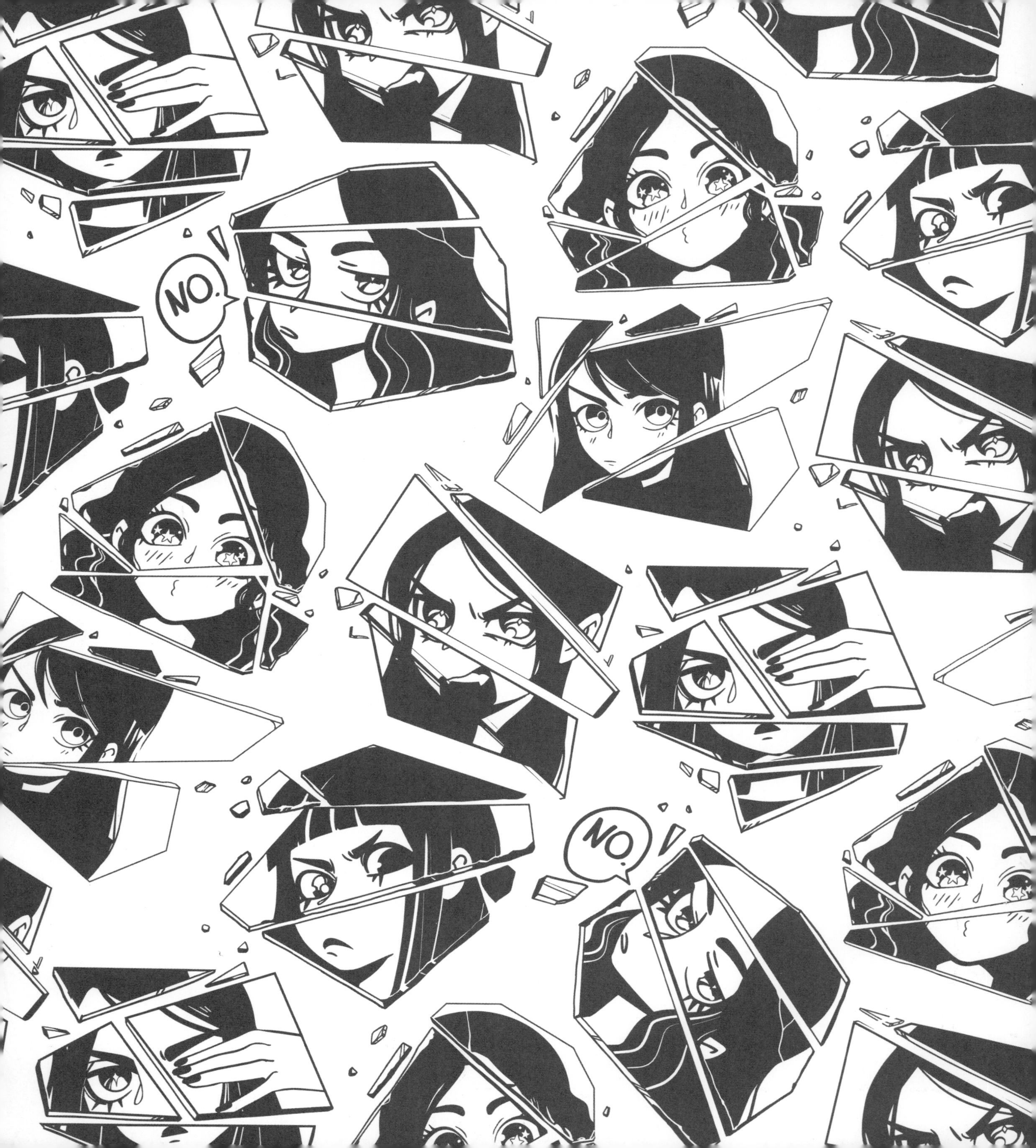
NO.
NO.

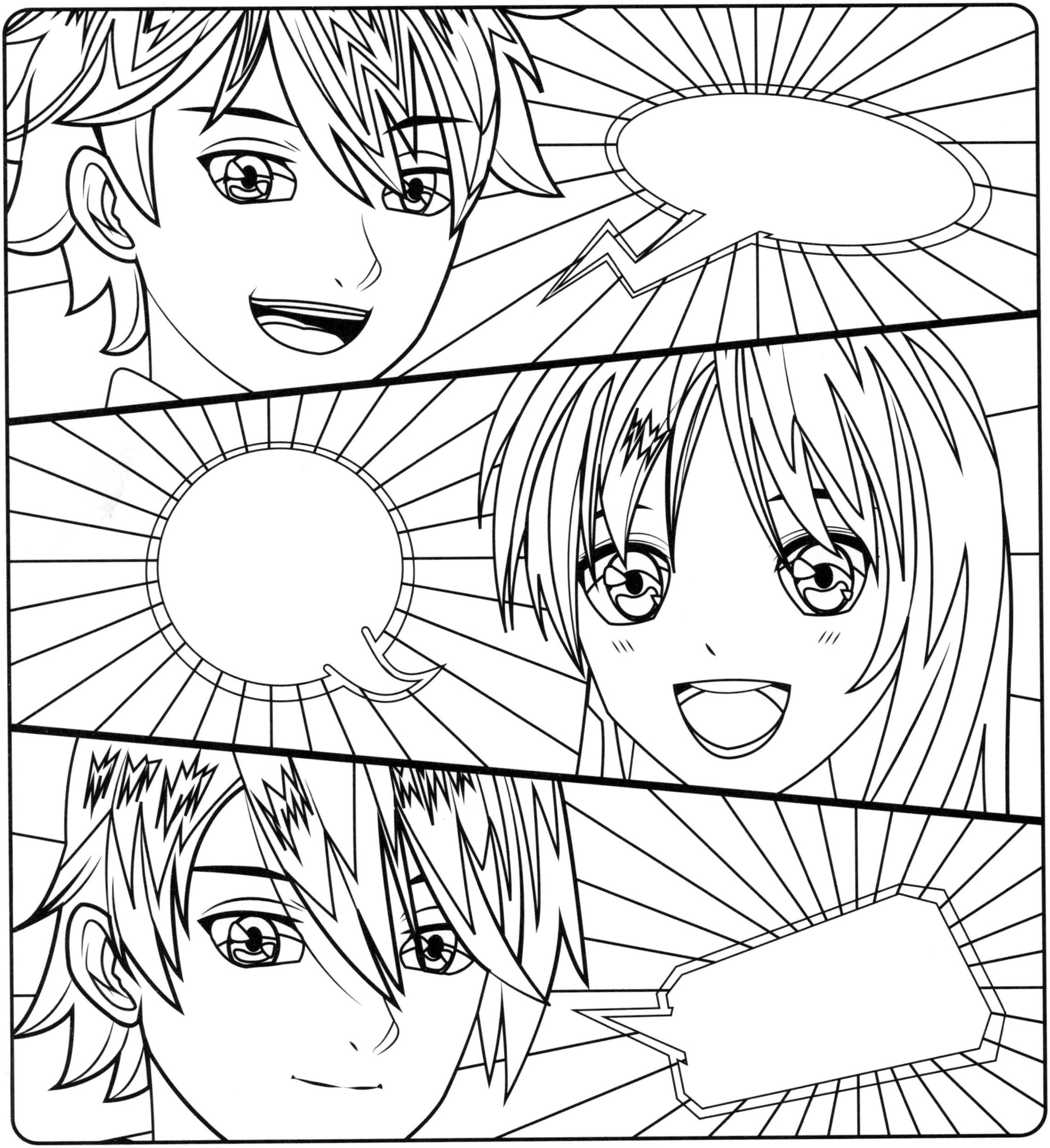

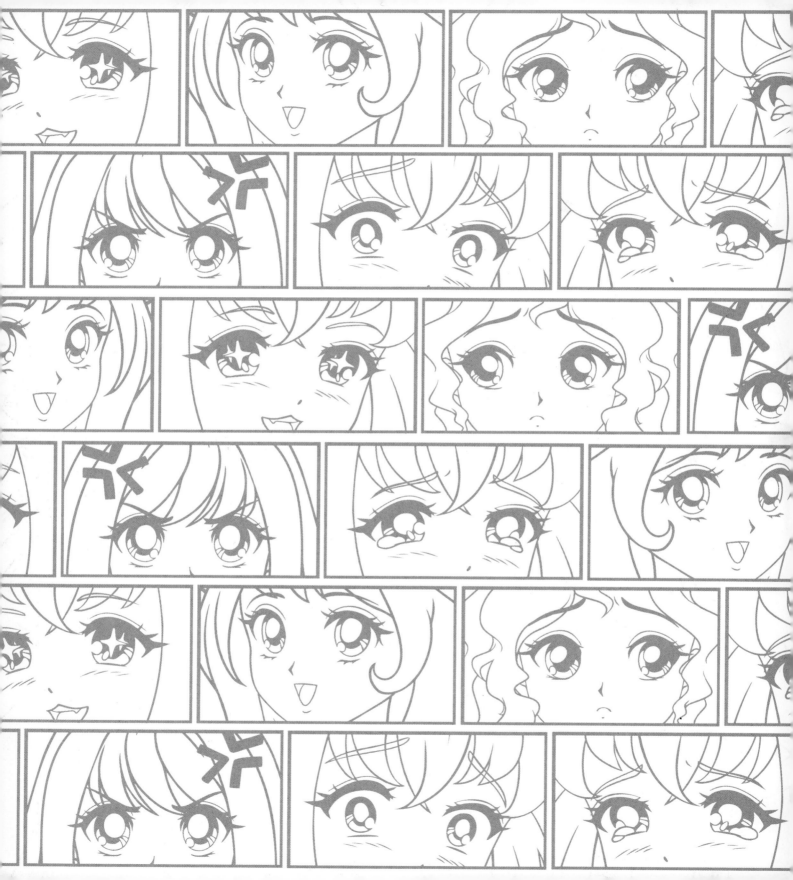

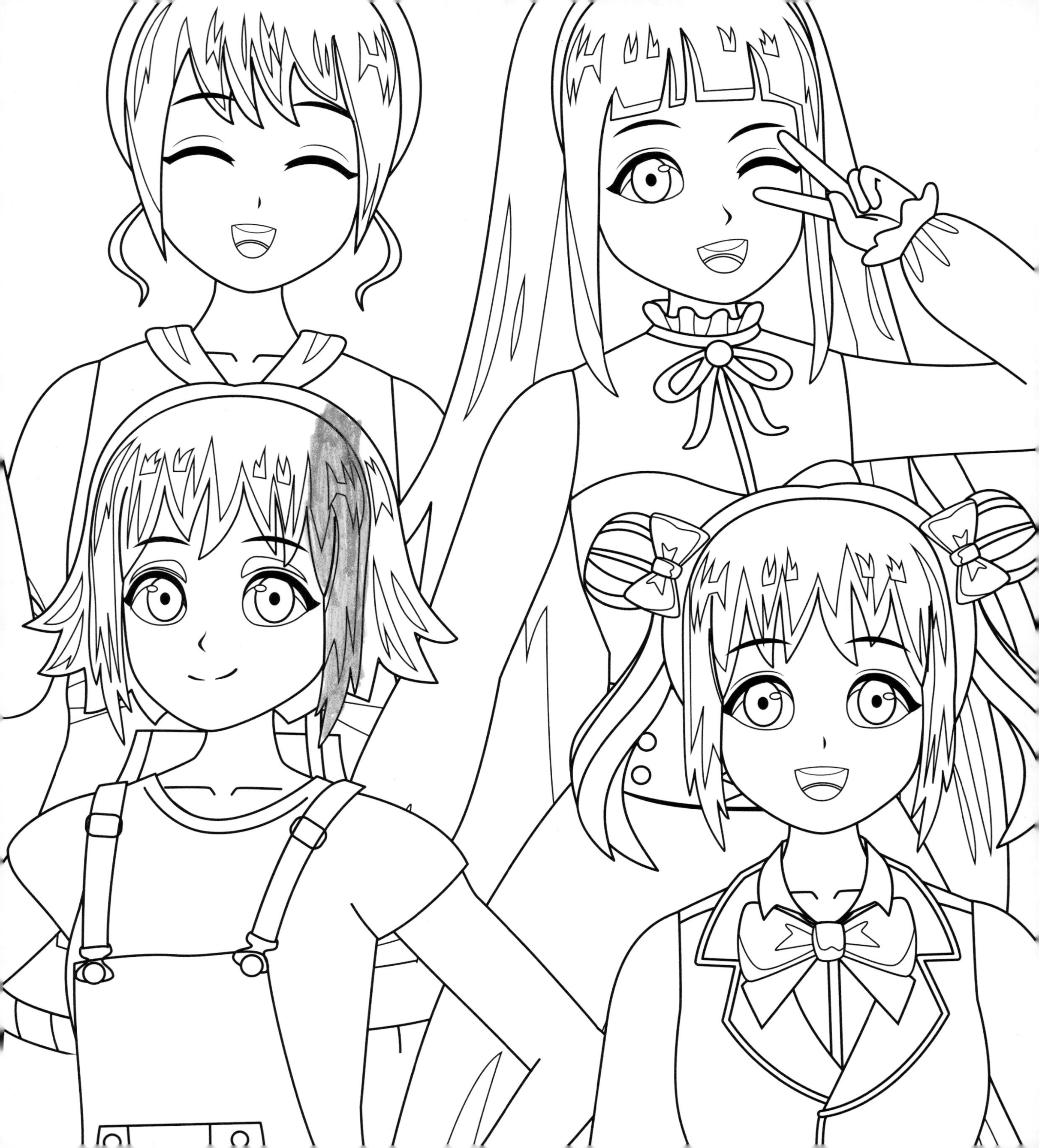

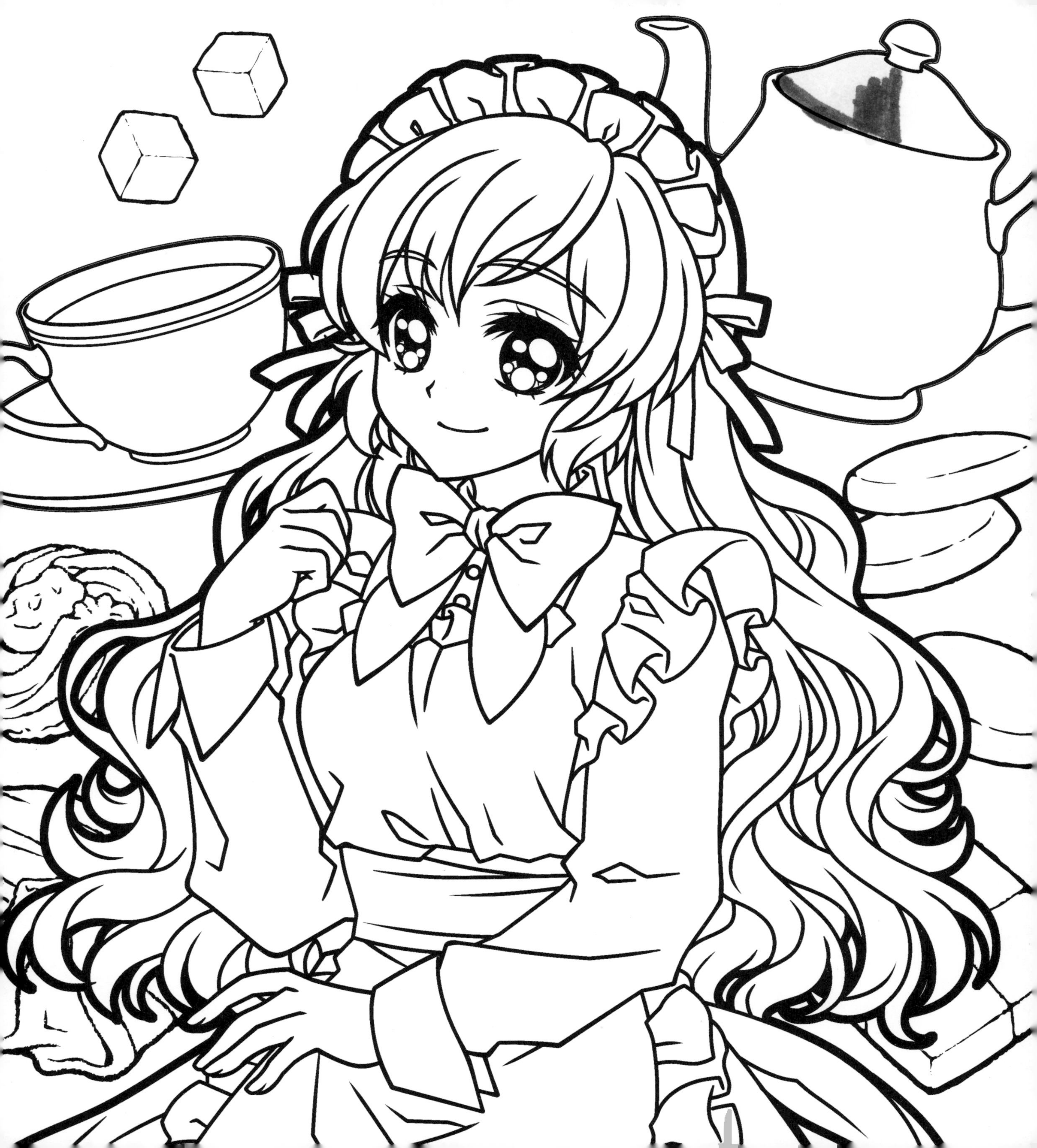

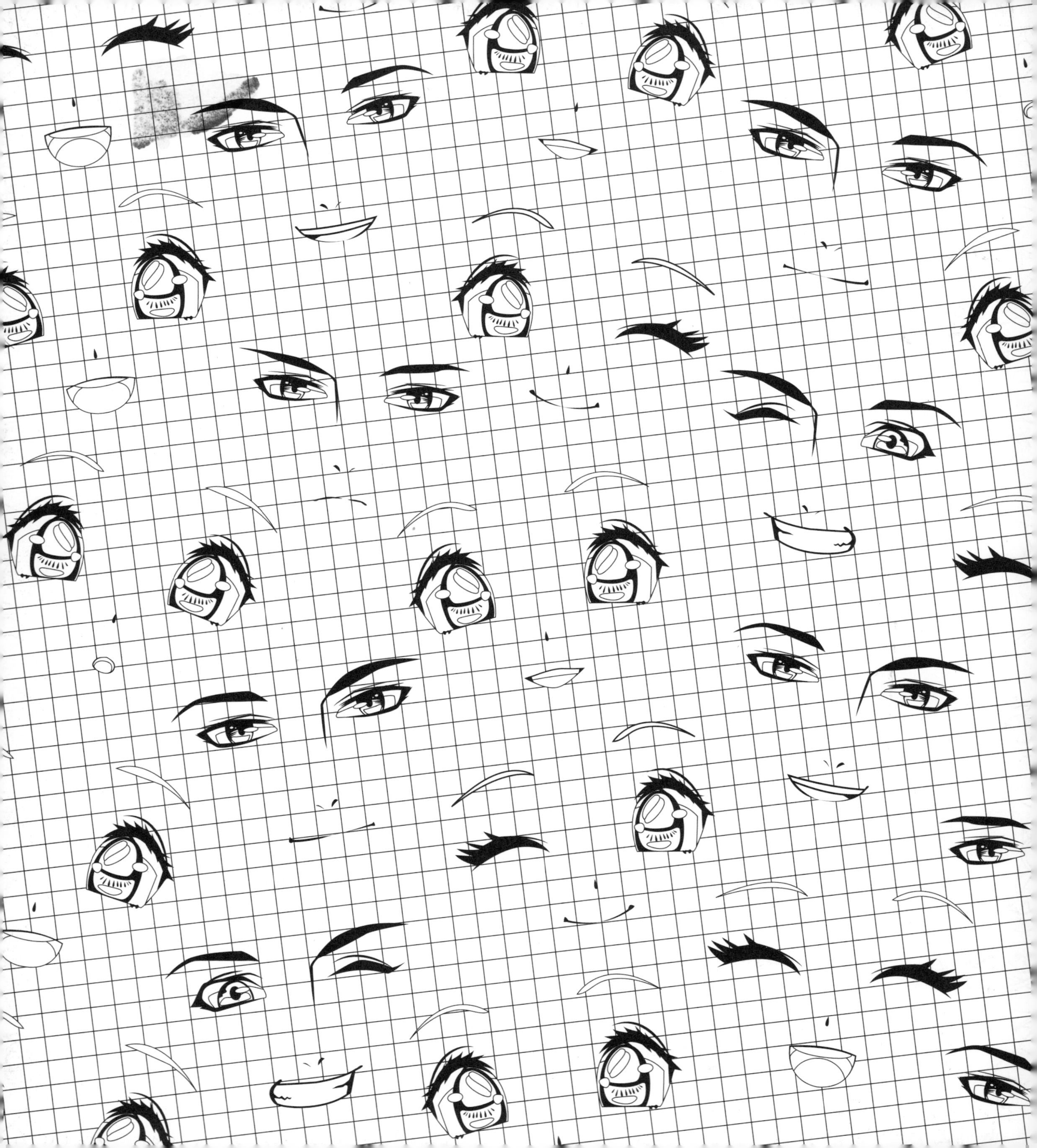

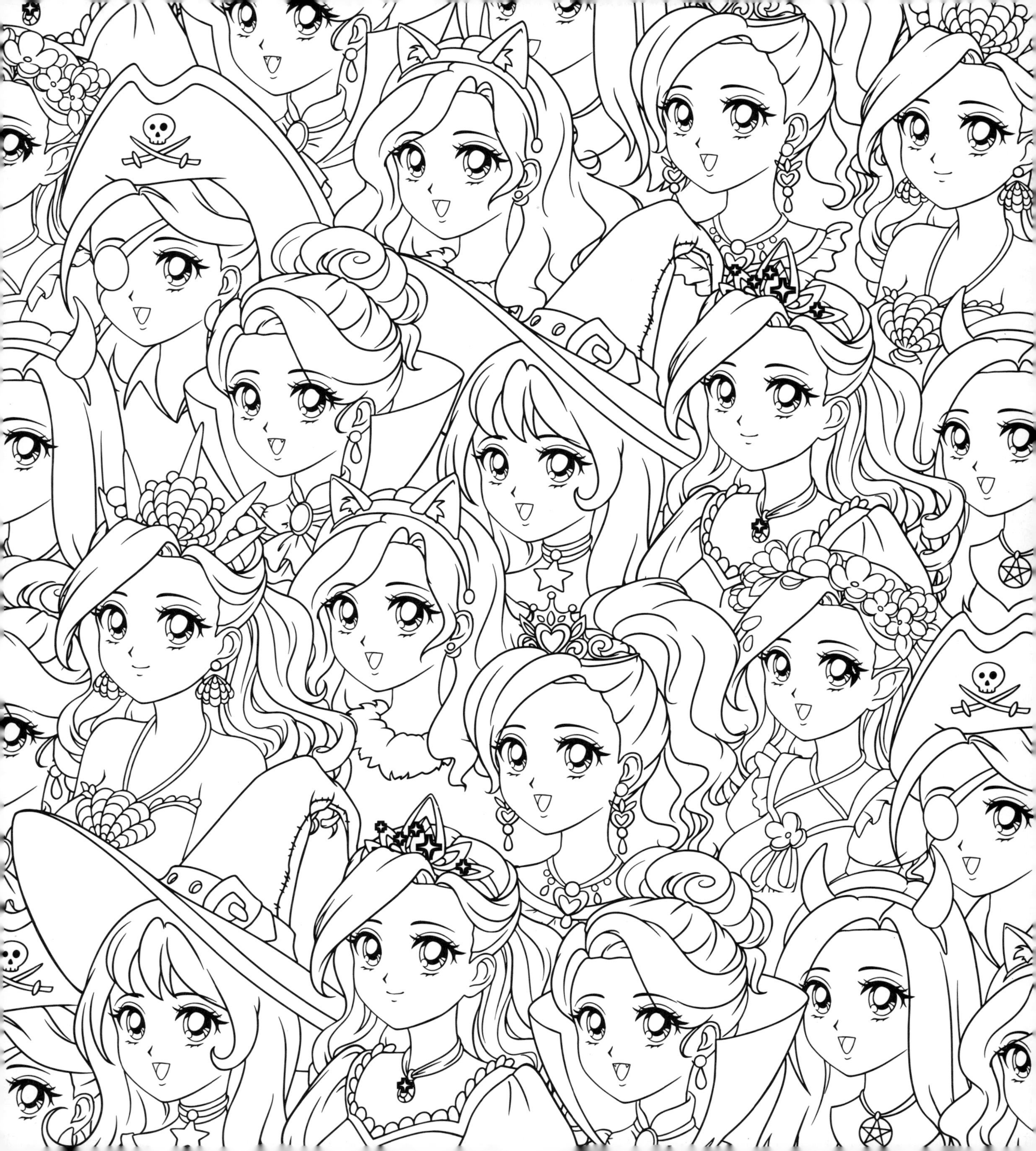

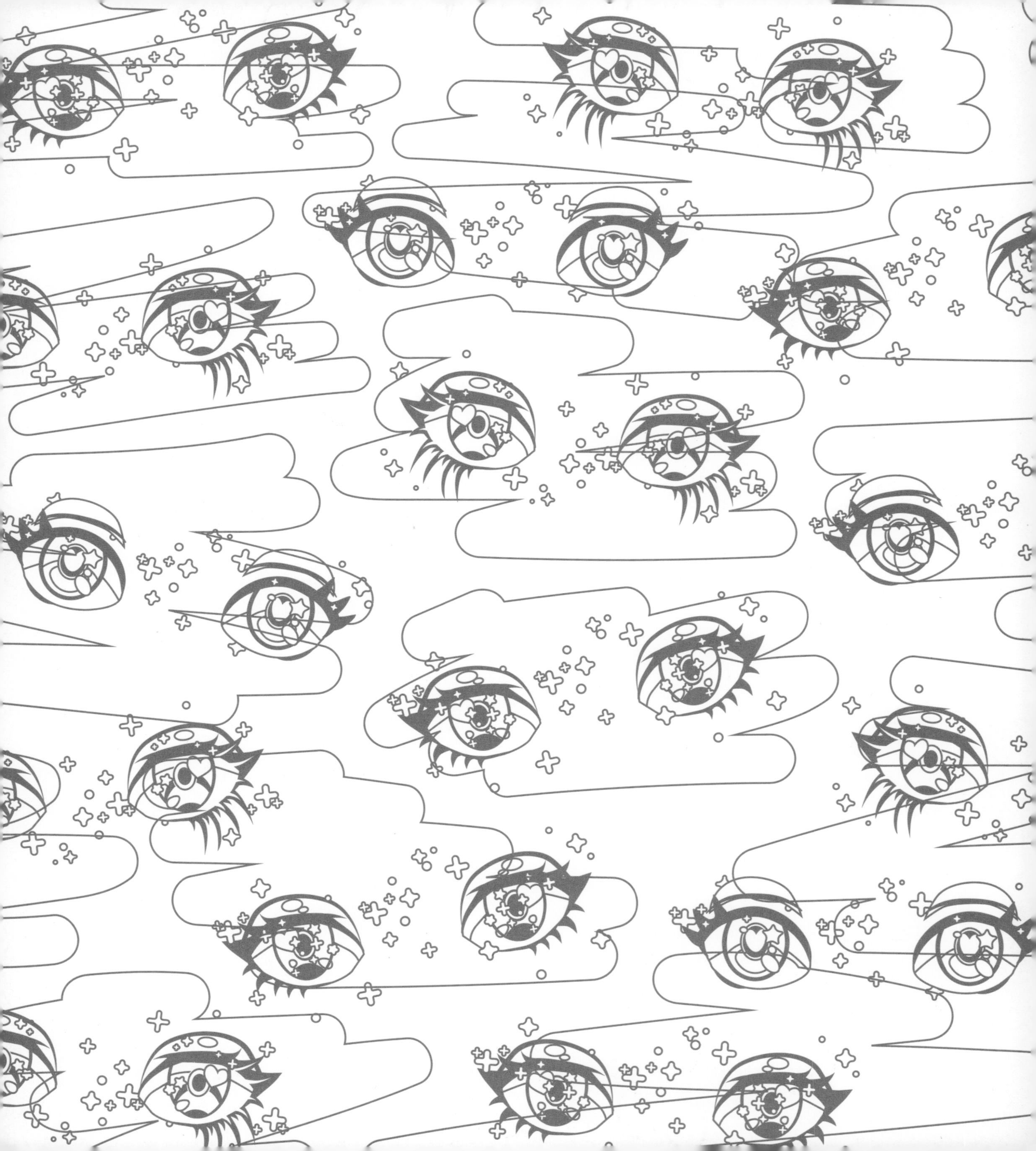

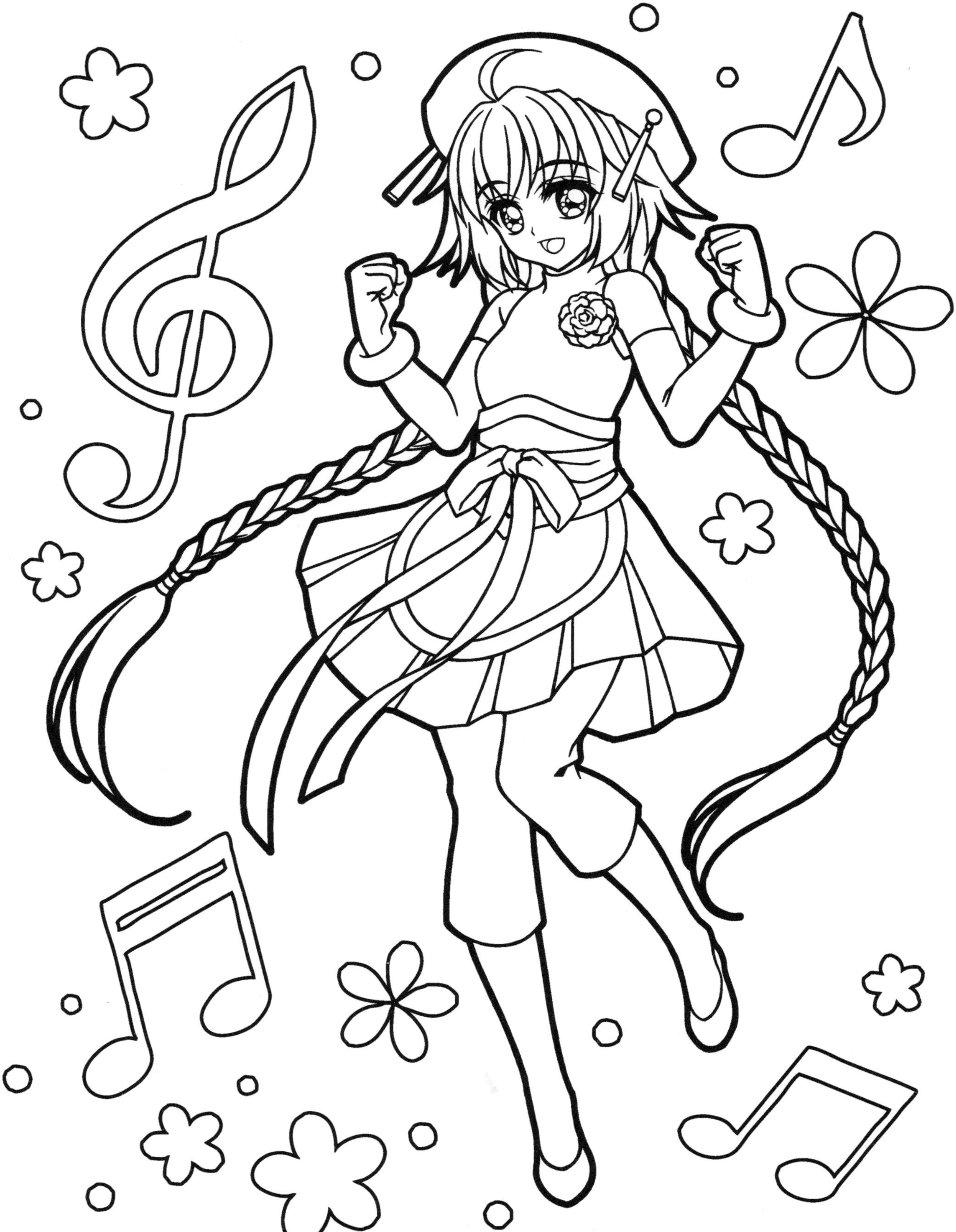

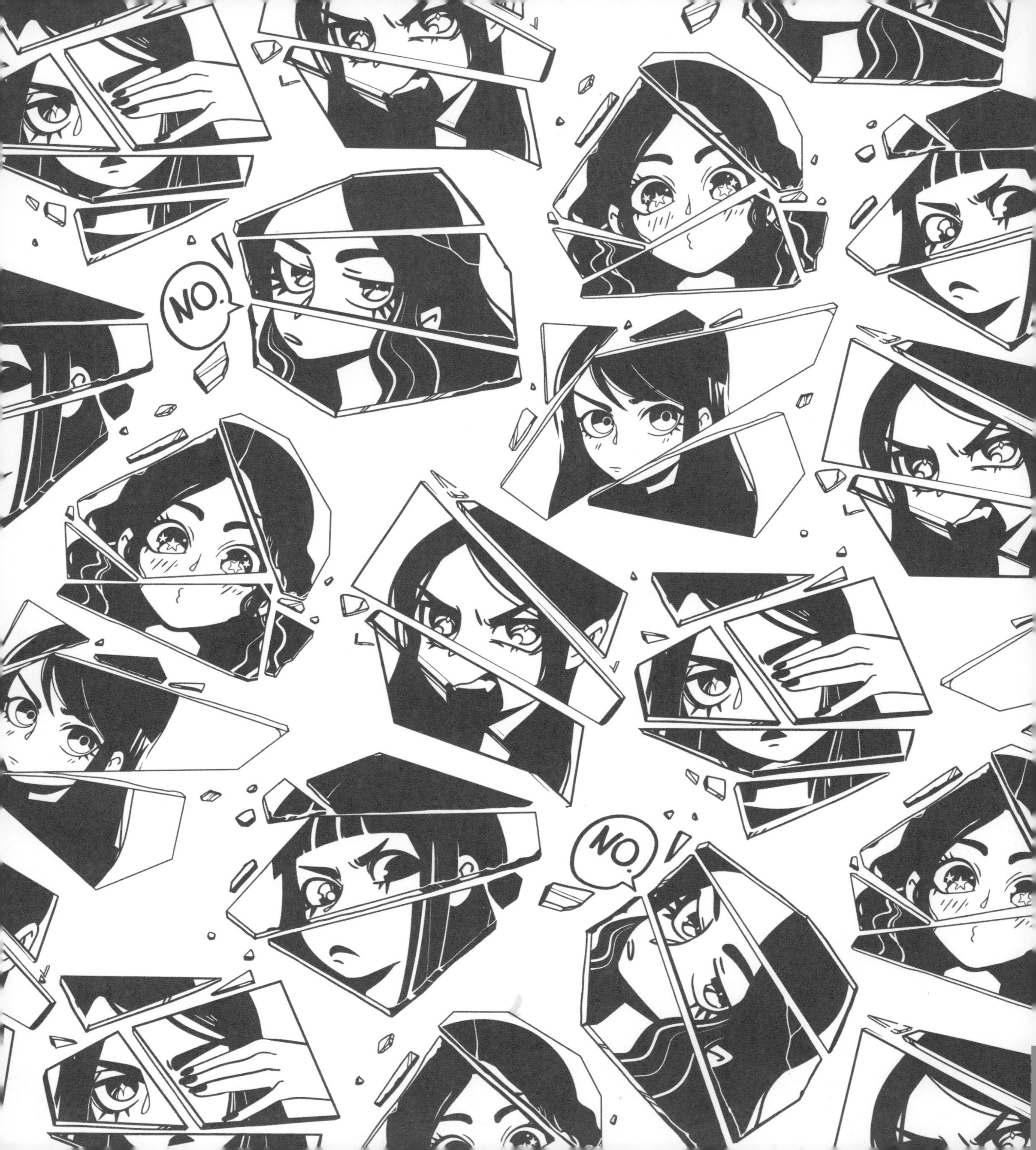
NO.
NO.

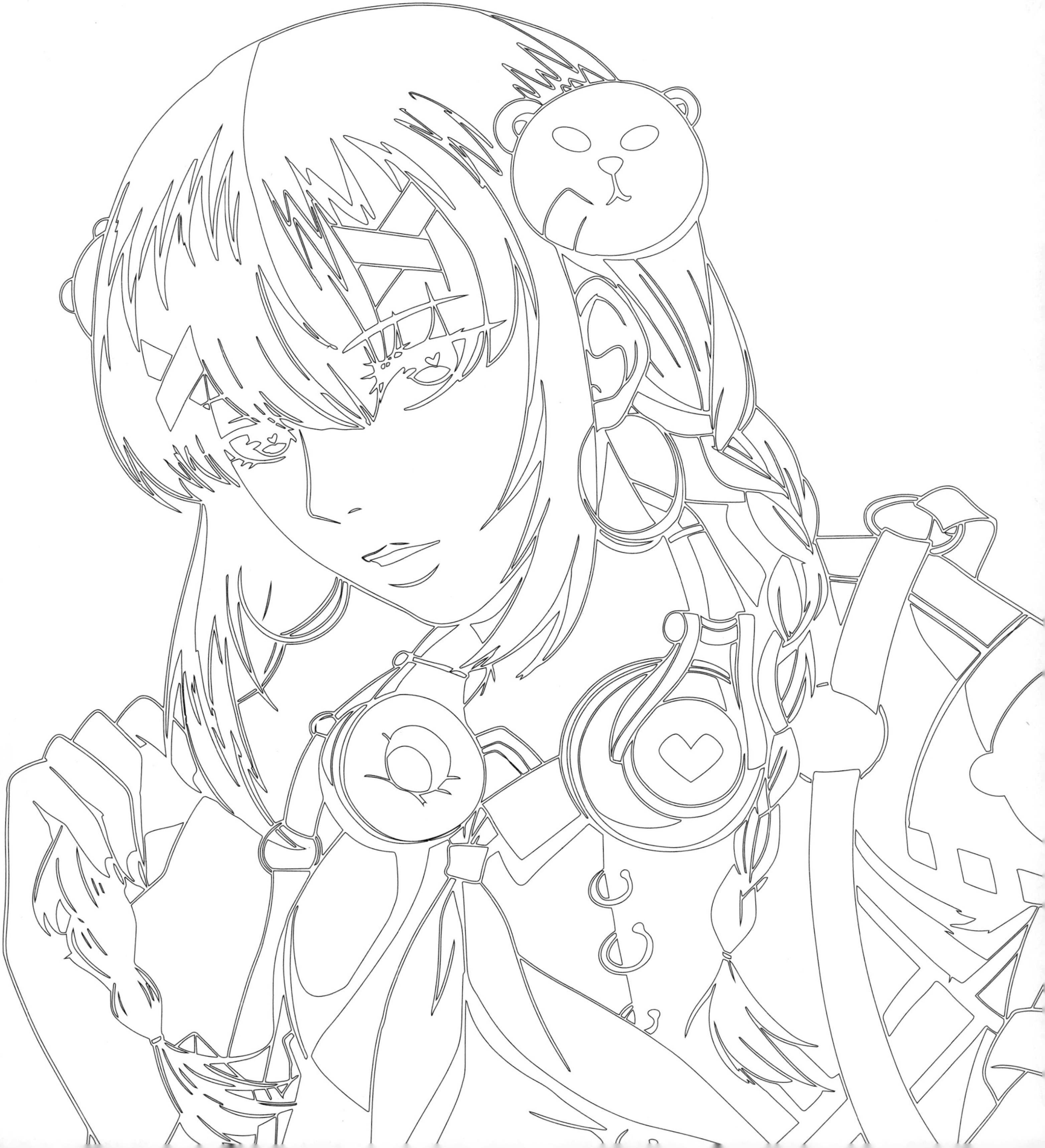

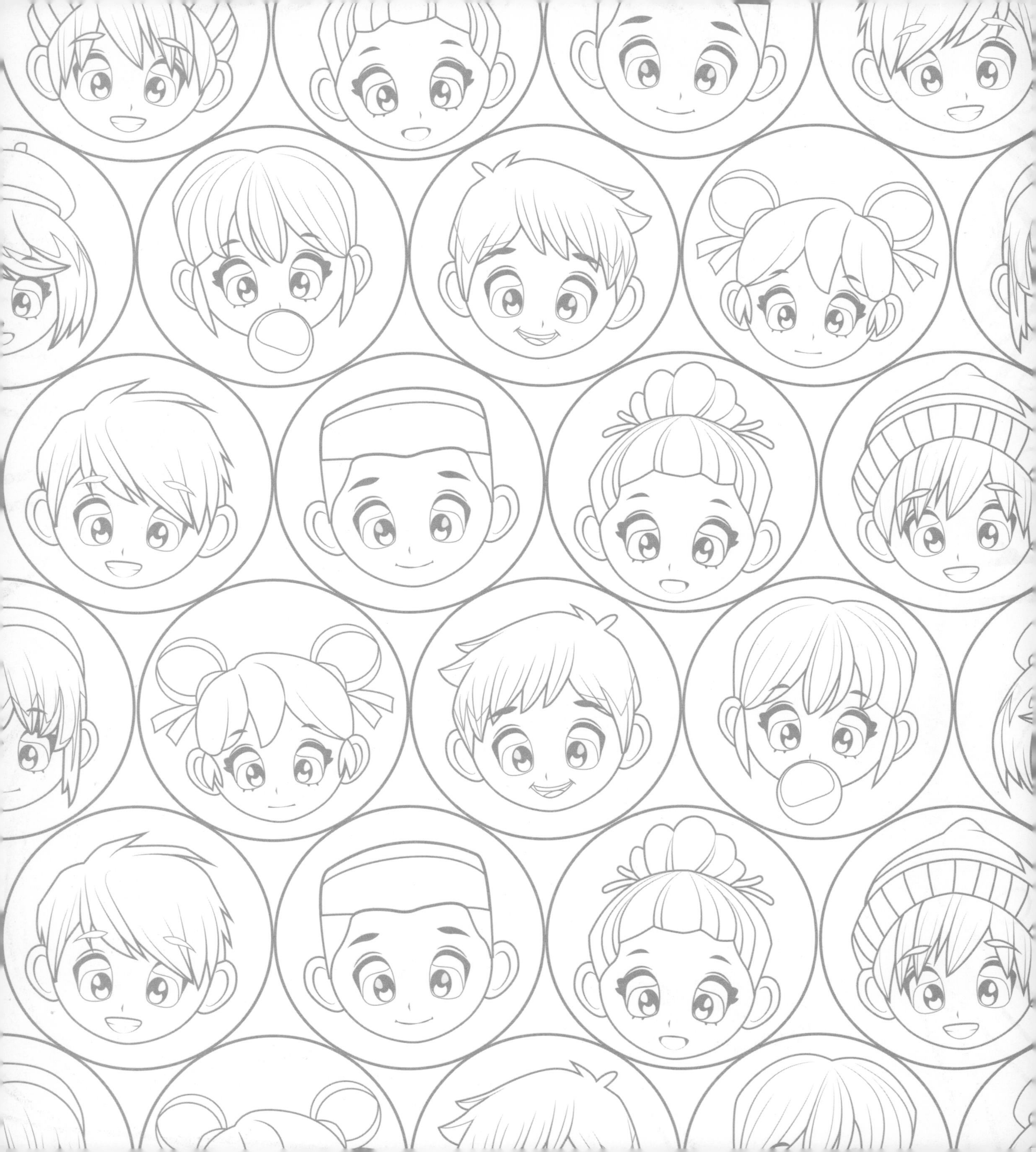

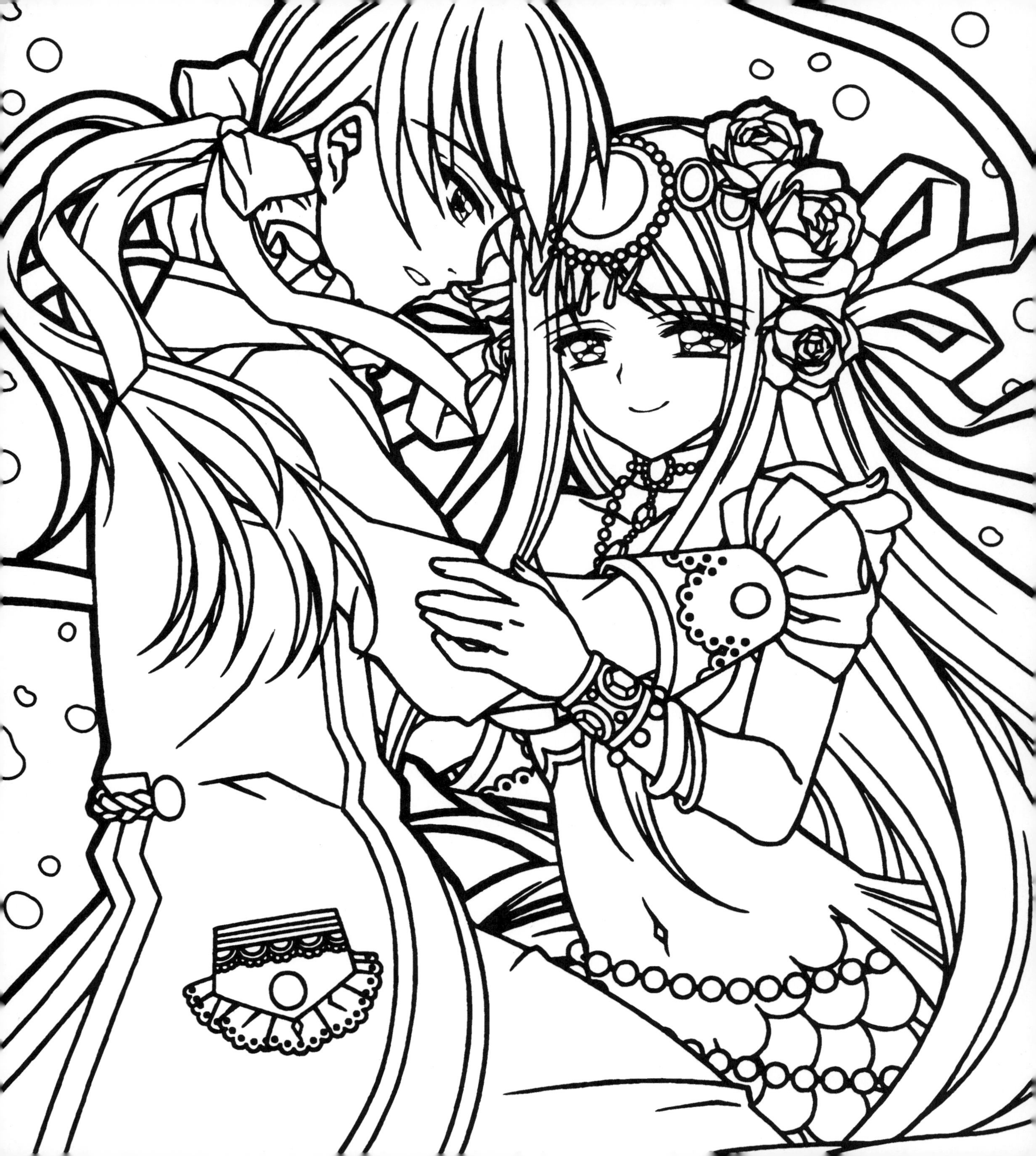

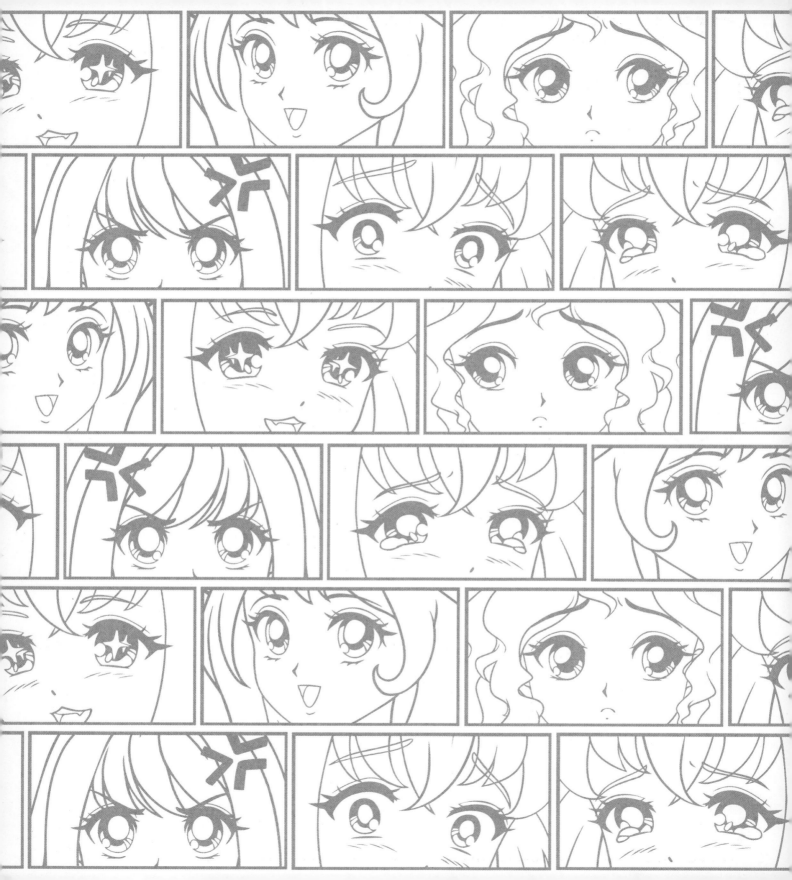

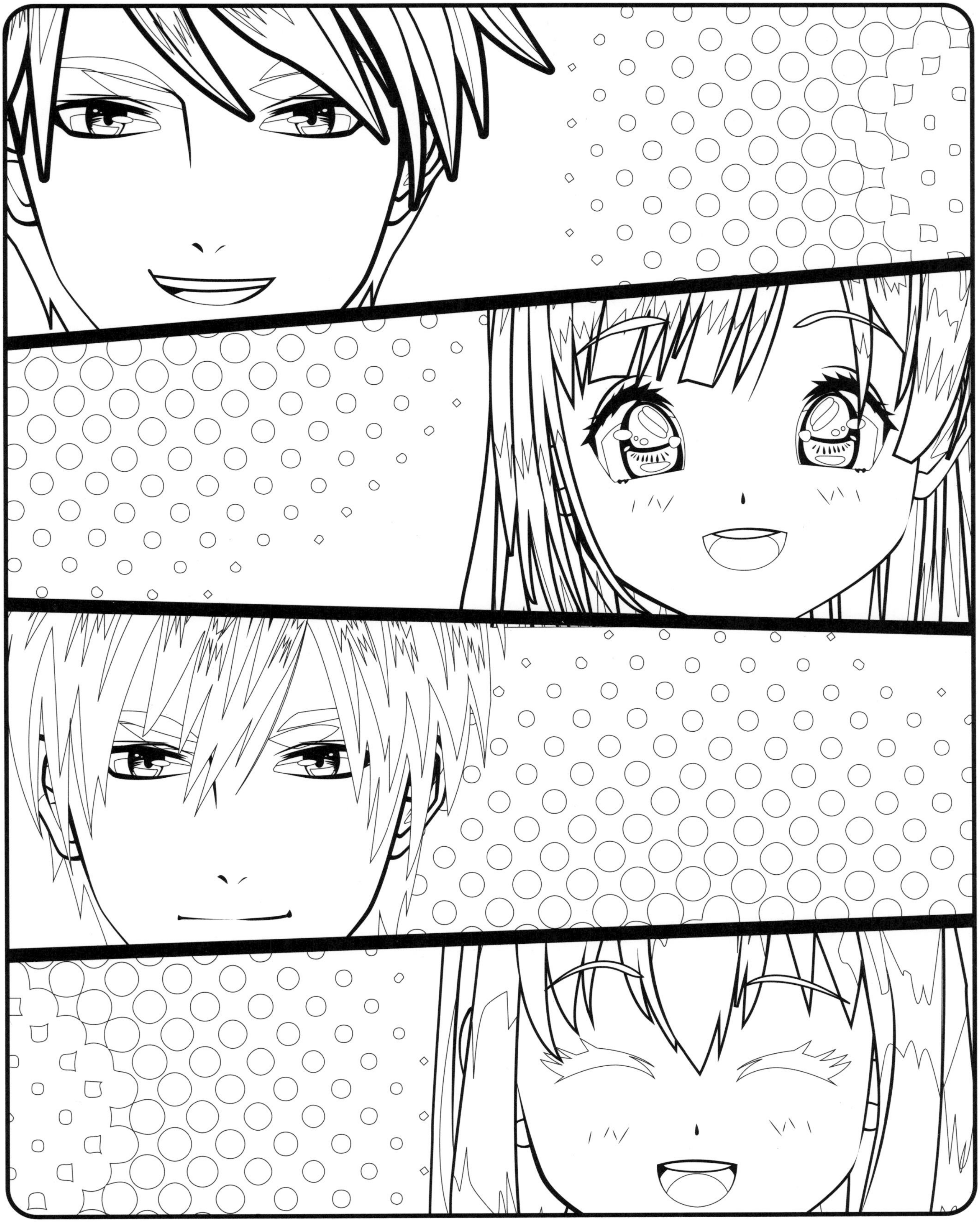

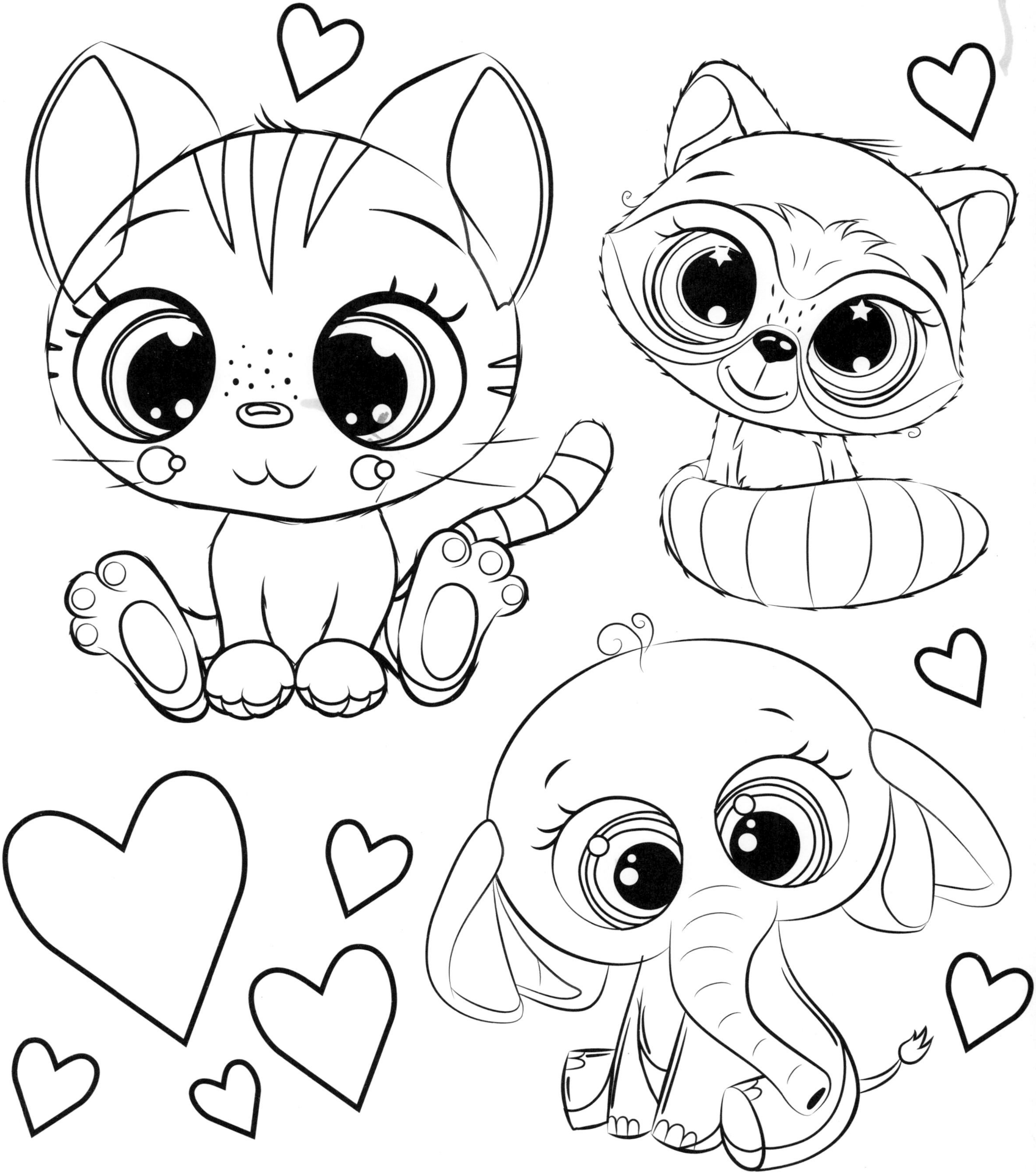

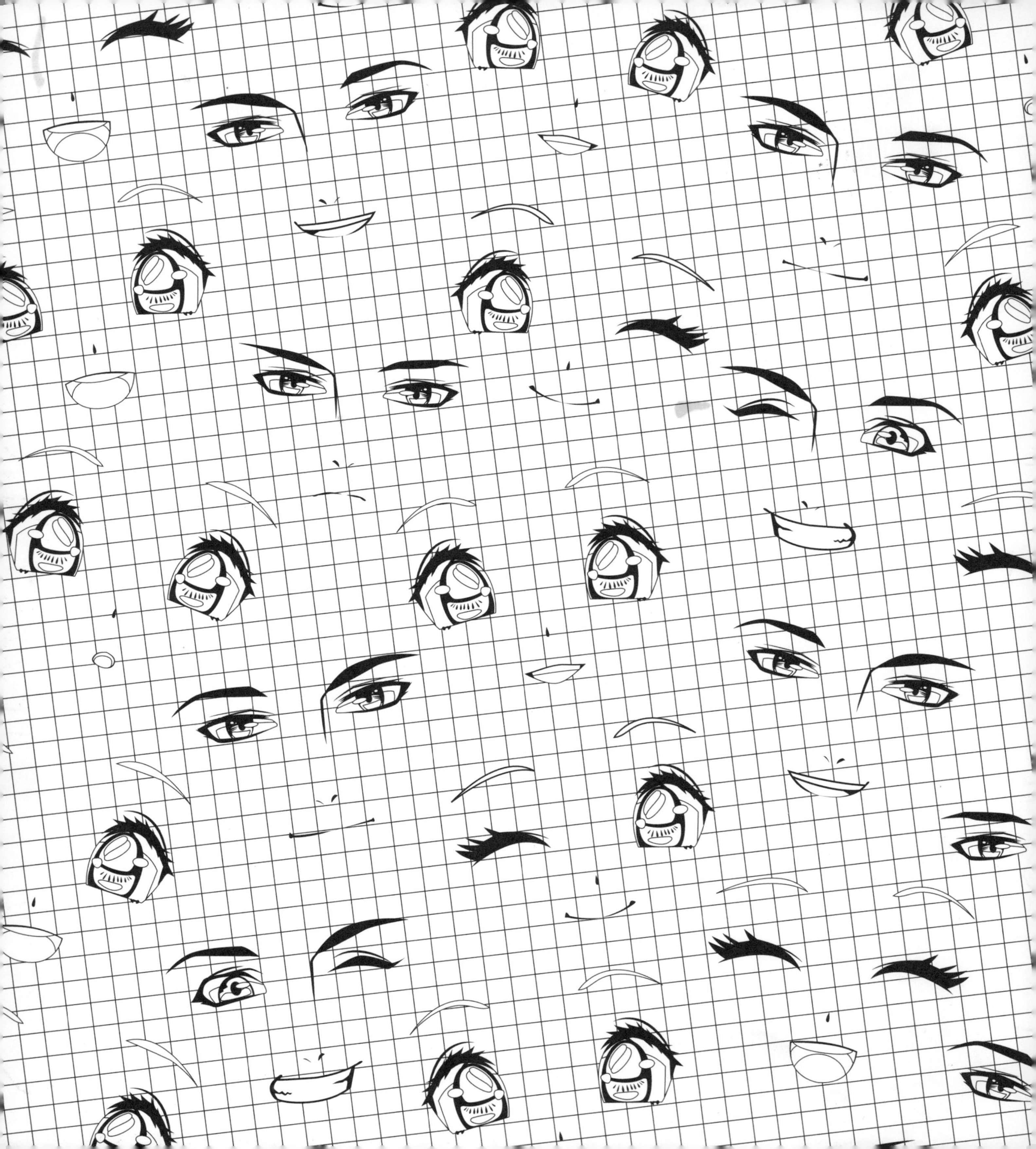

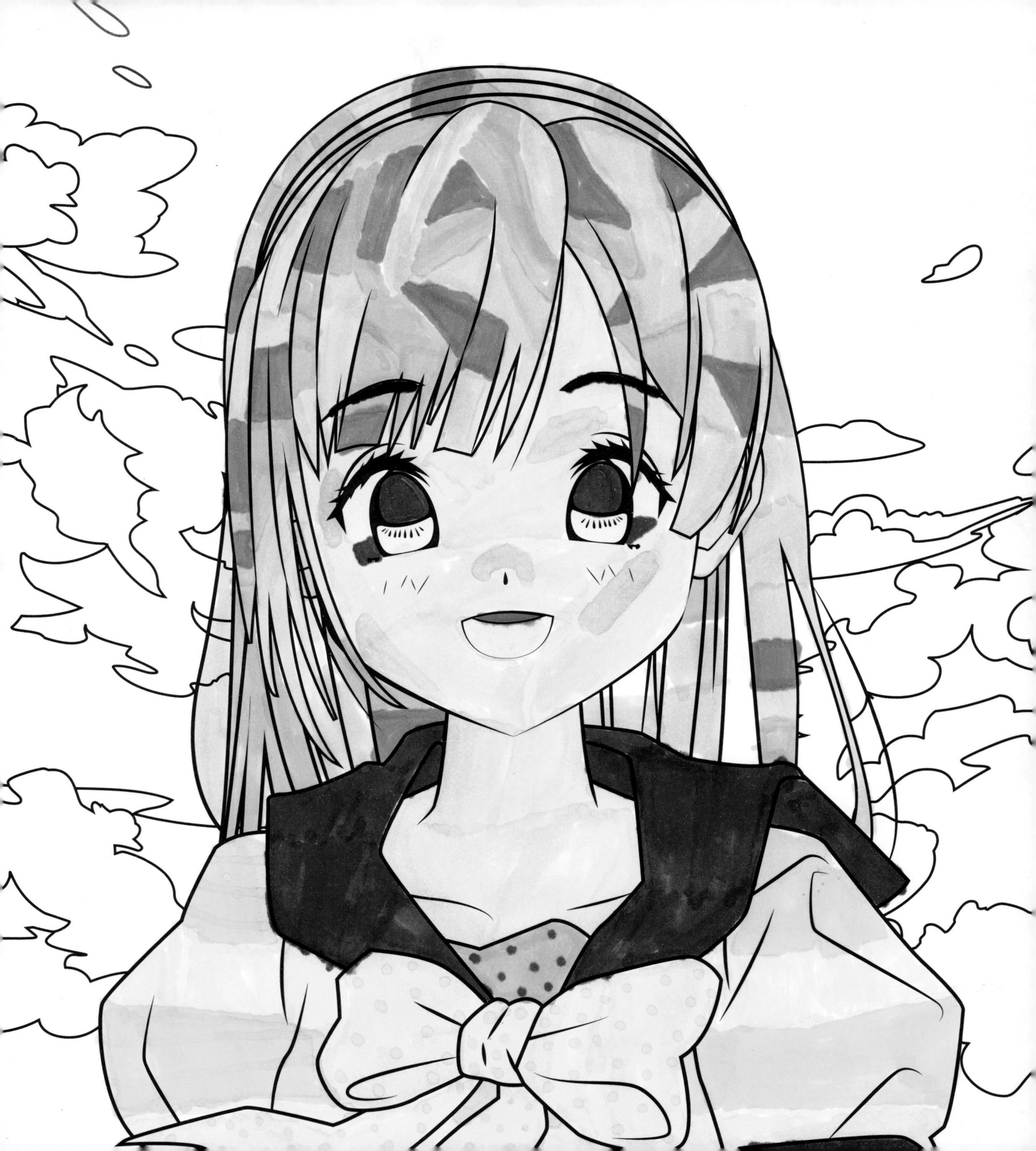

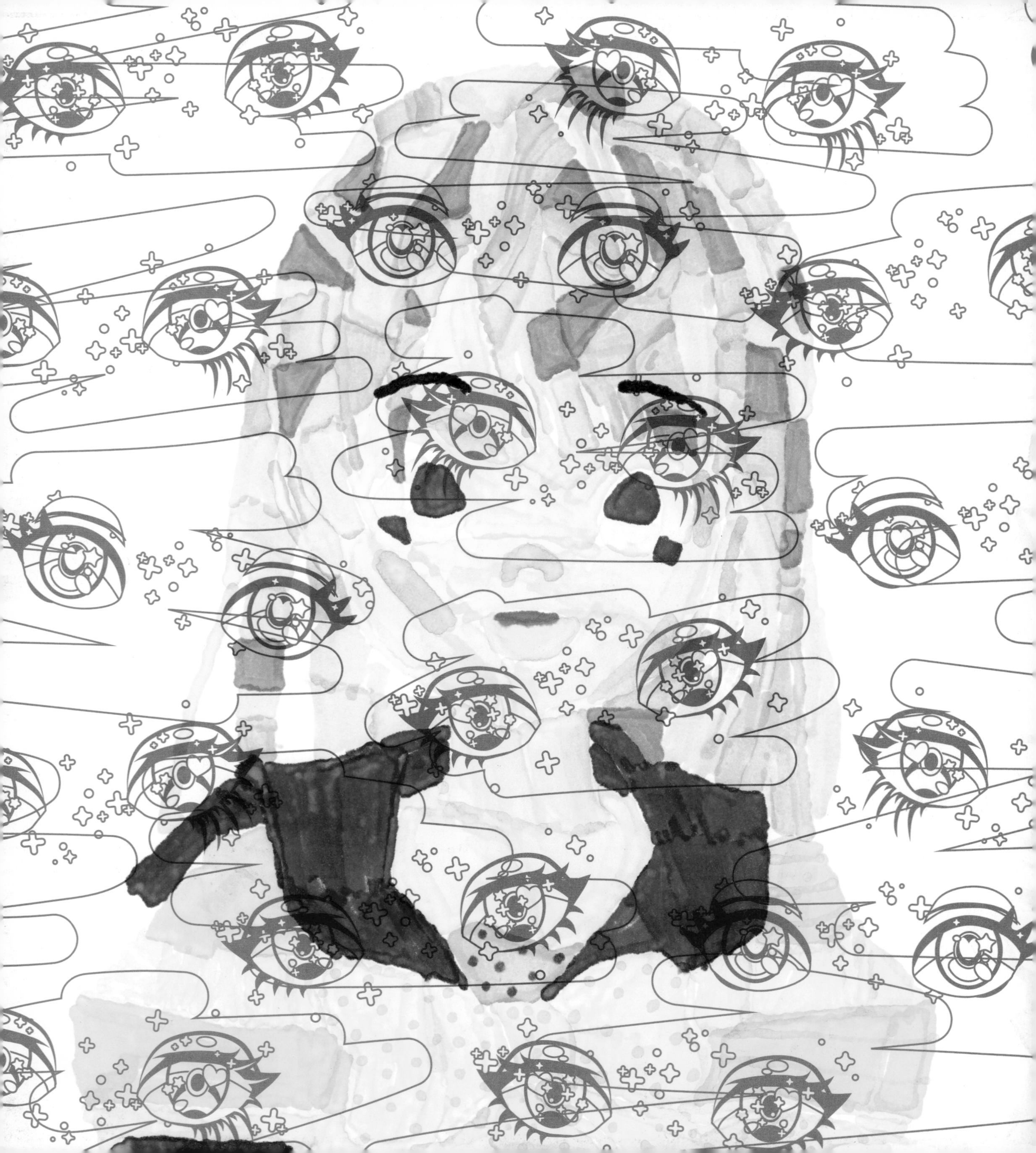

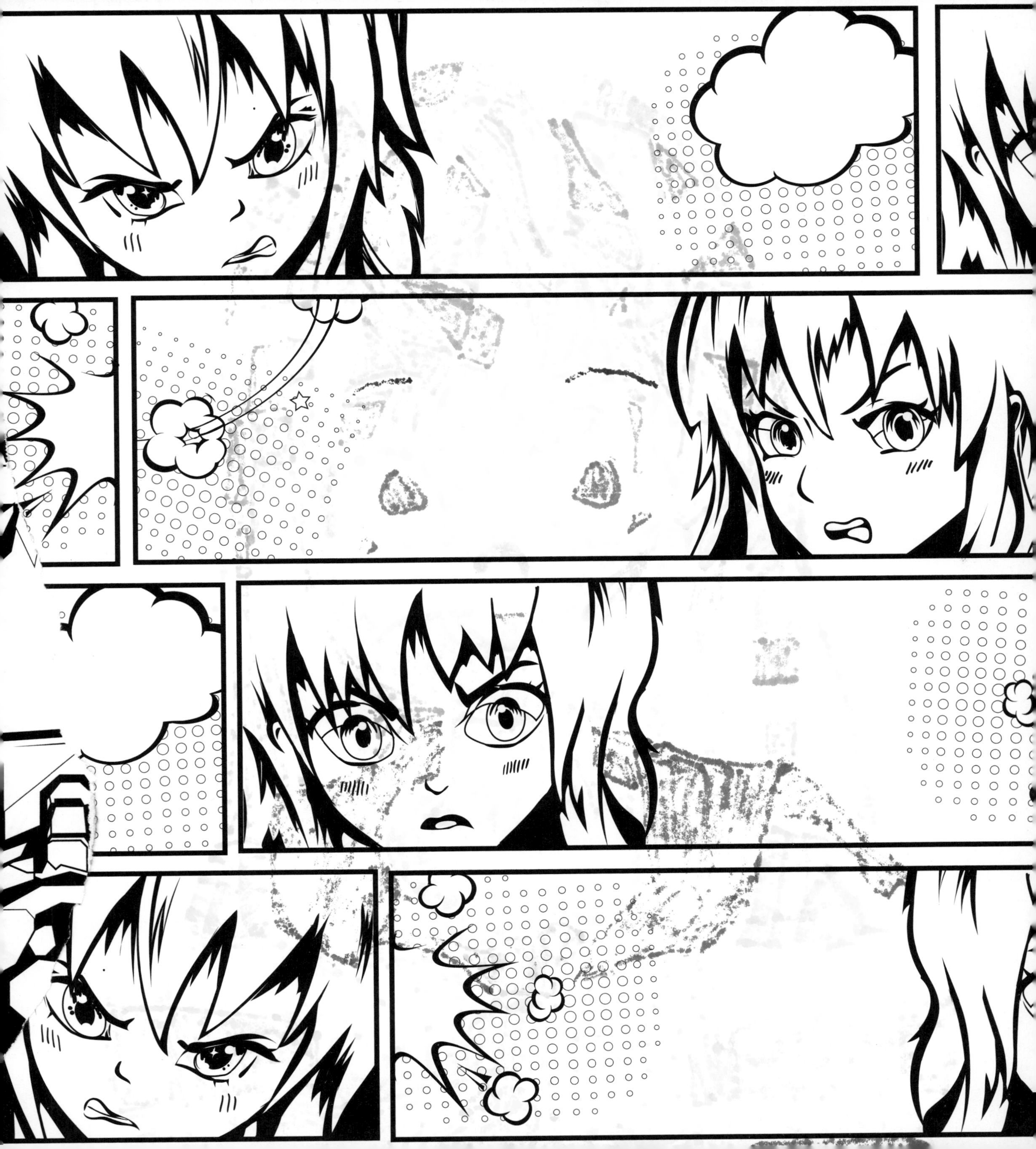

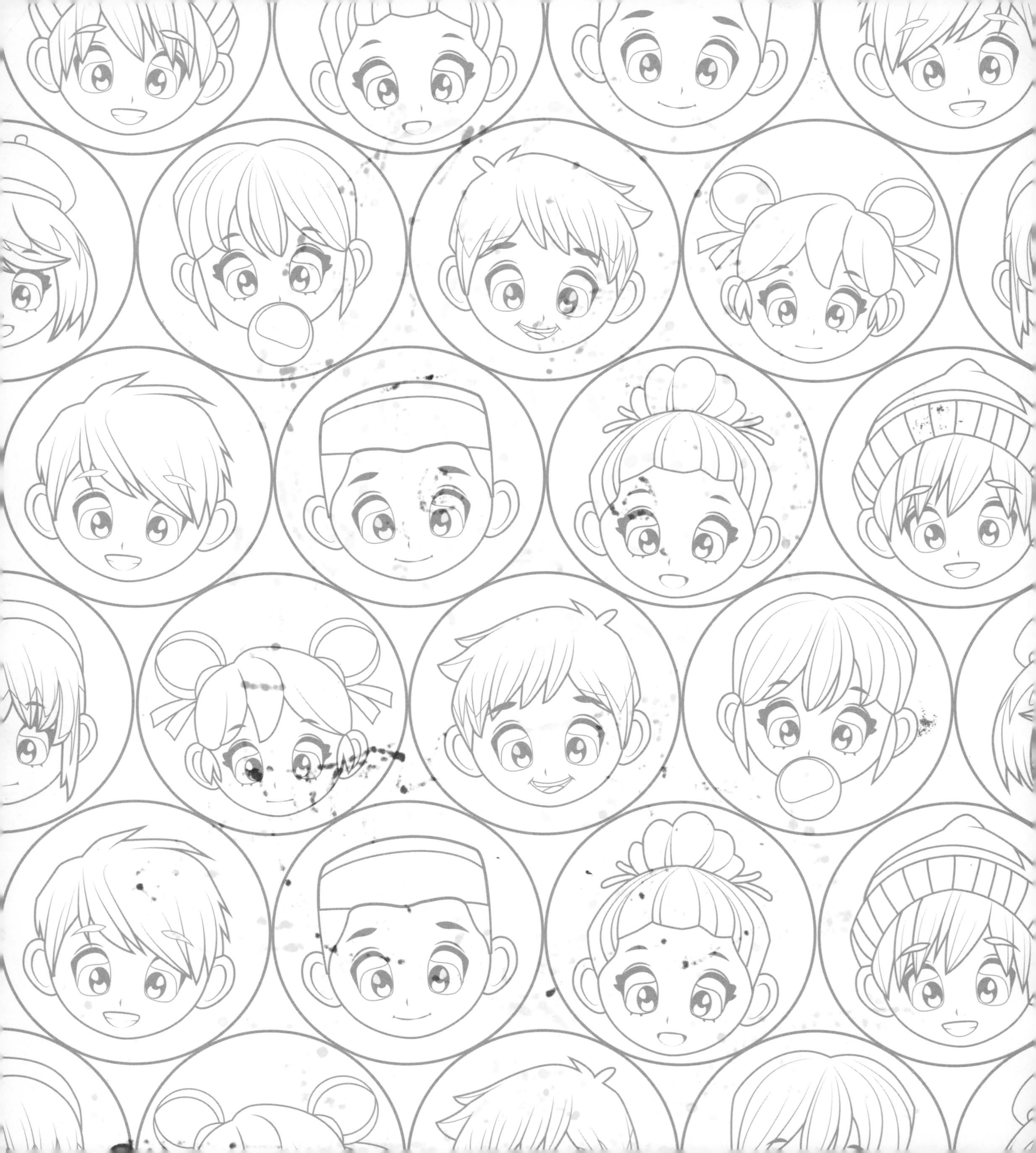

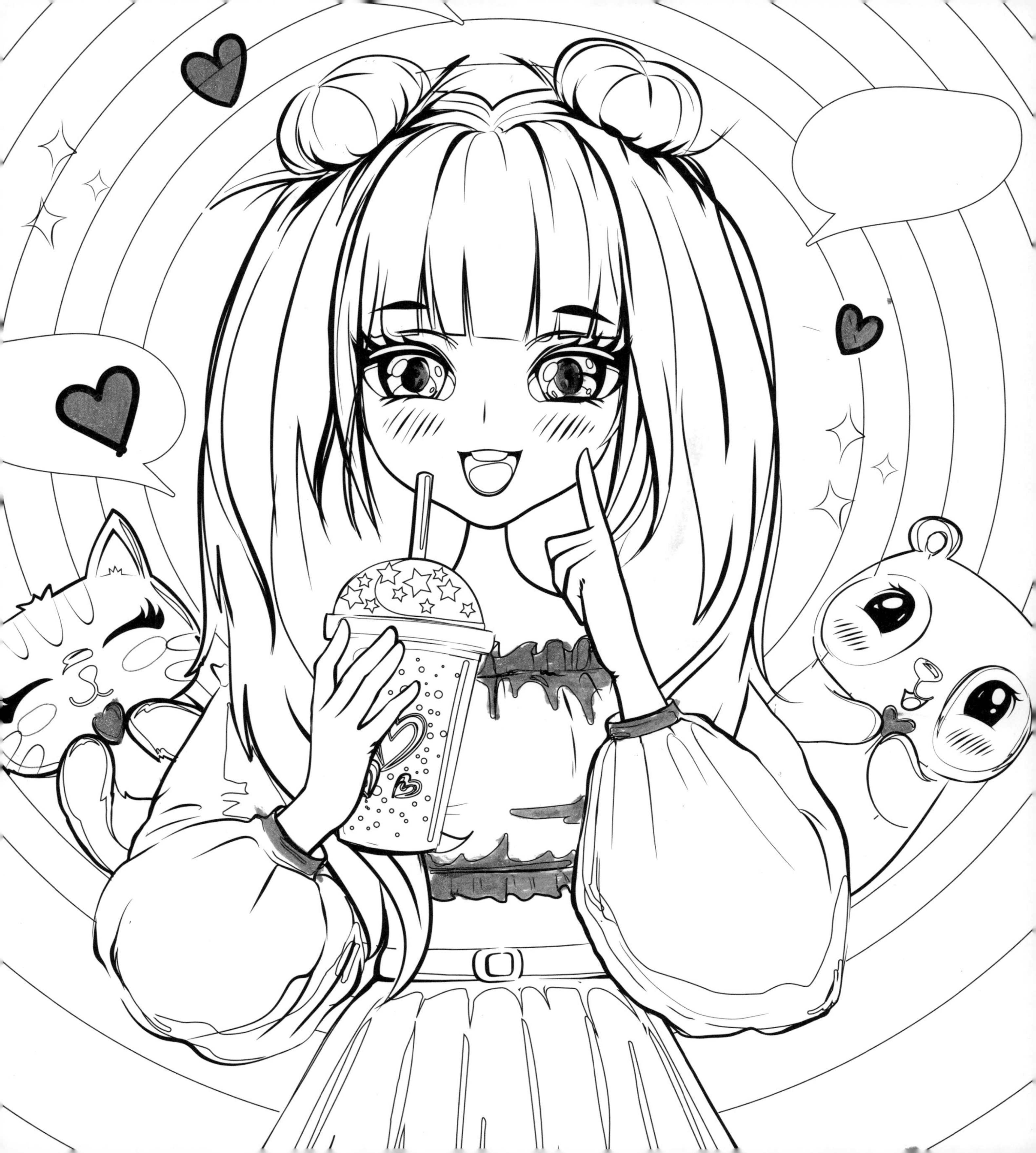

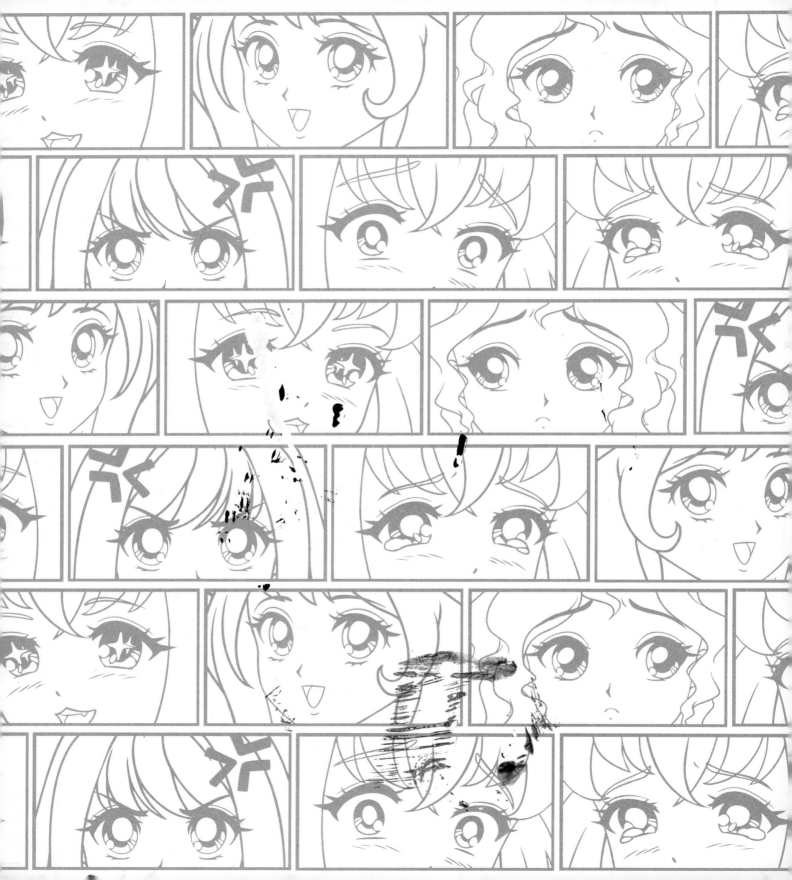

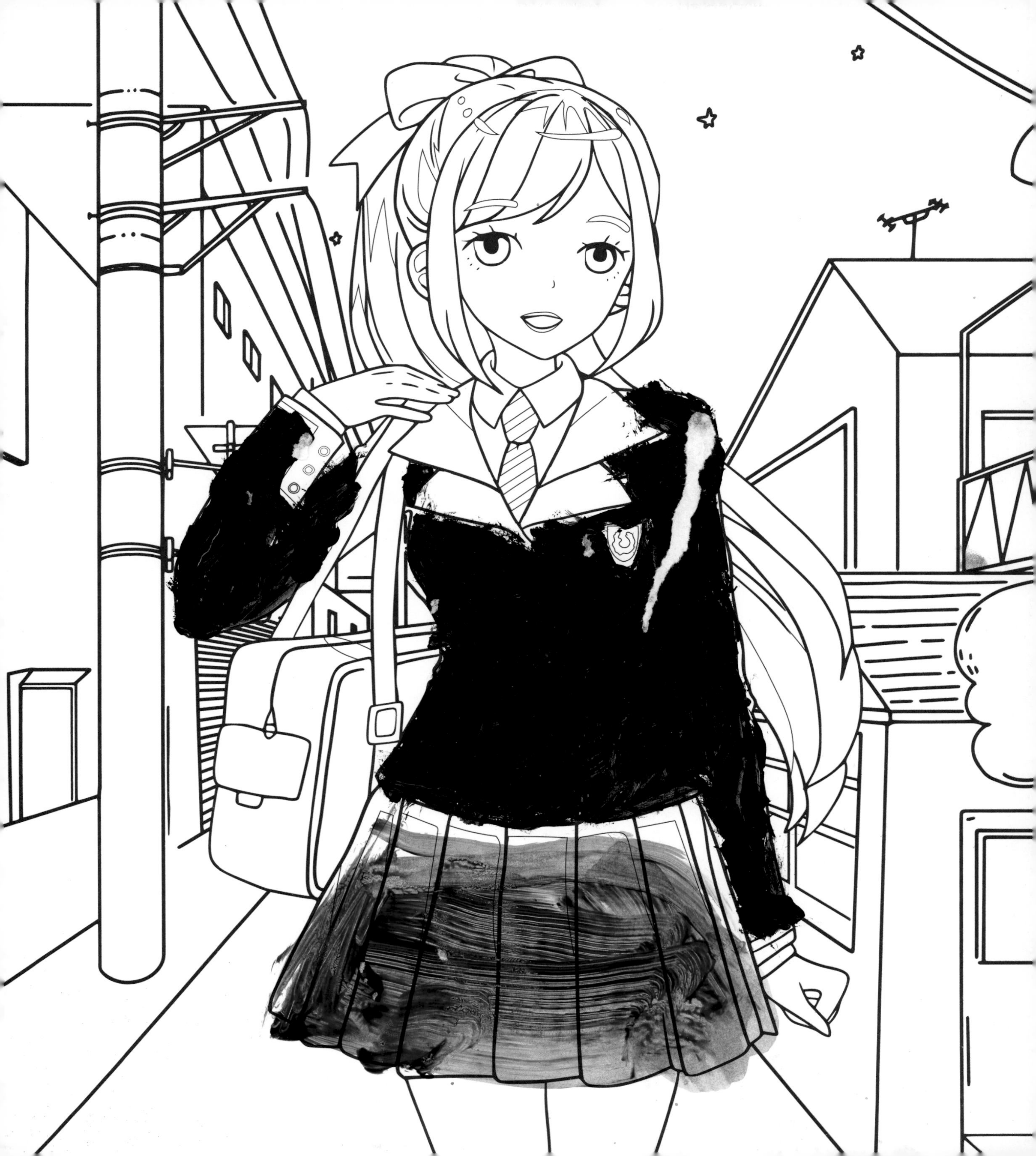

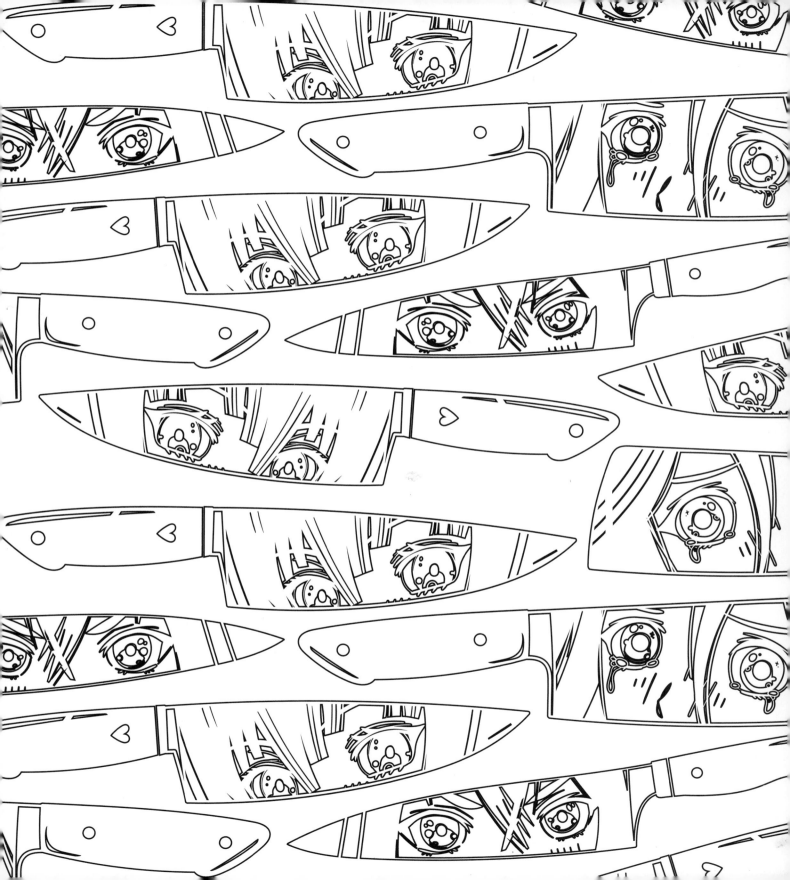

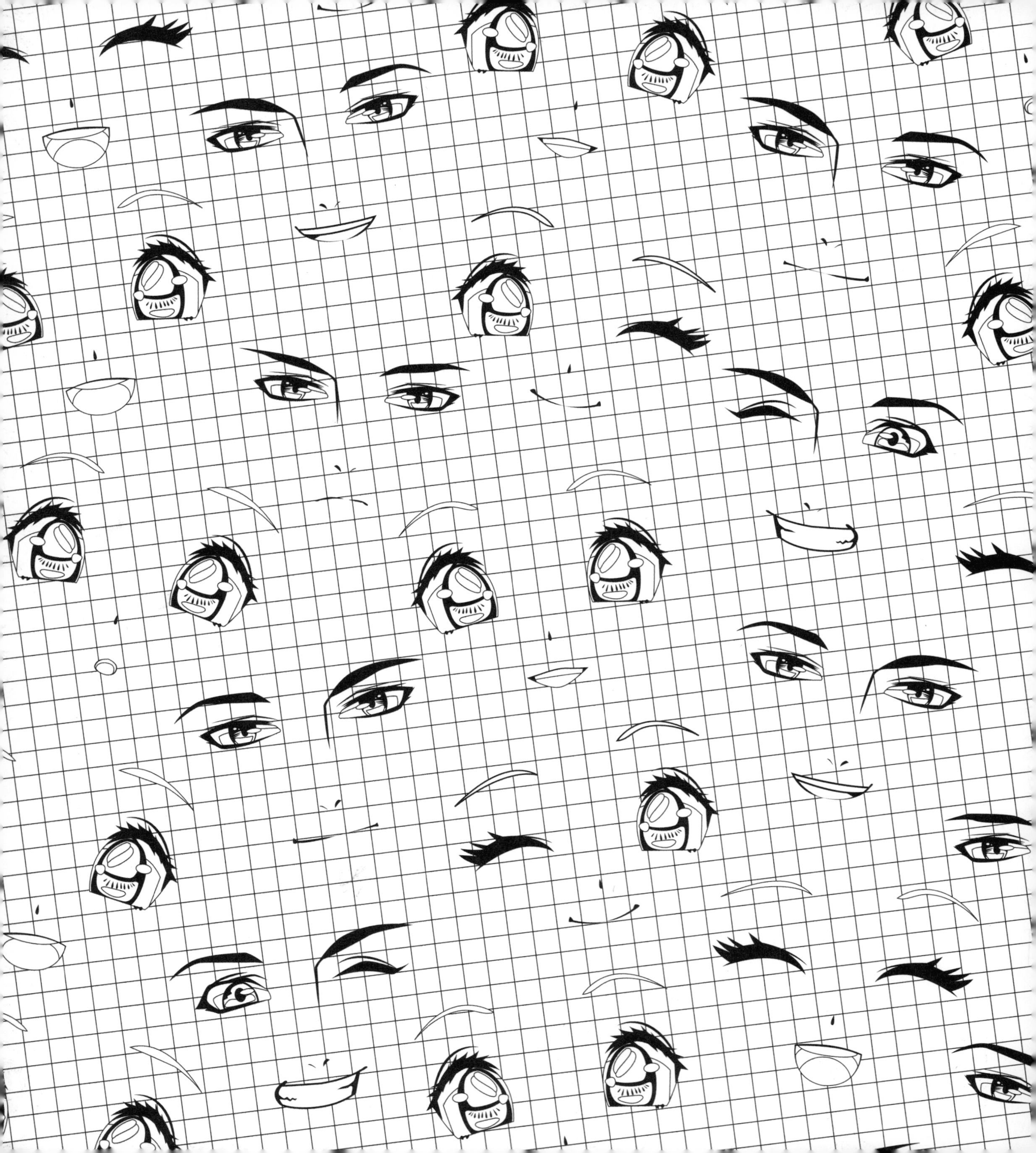

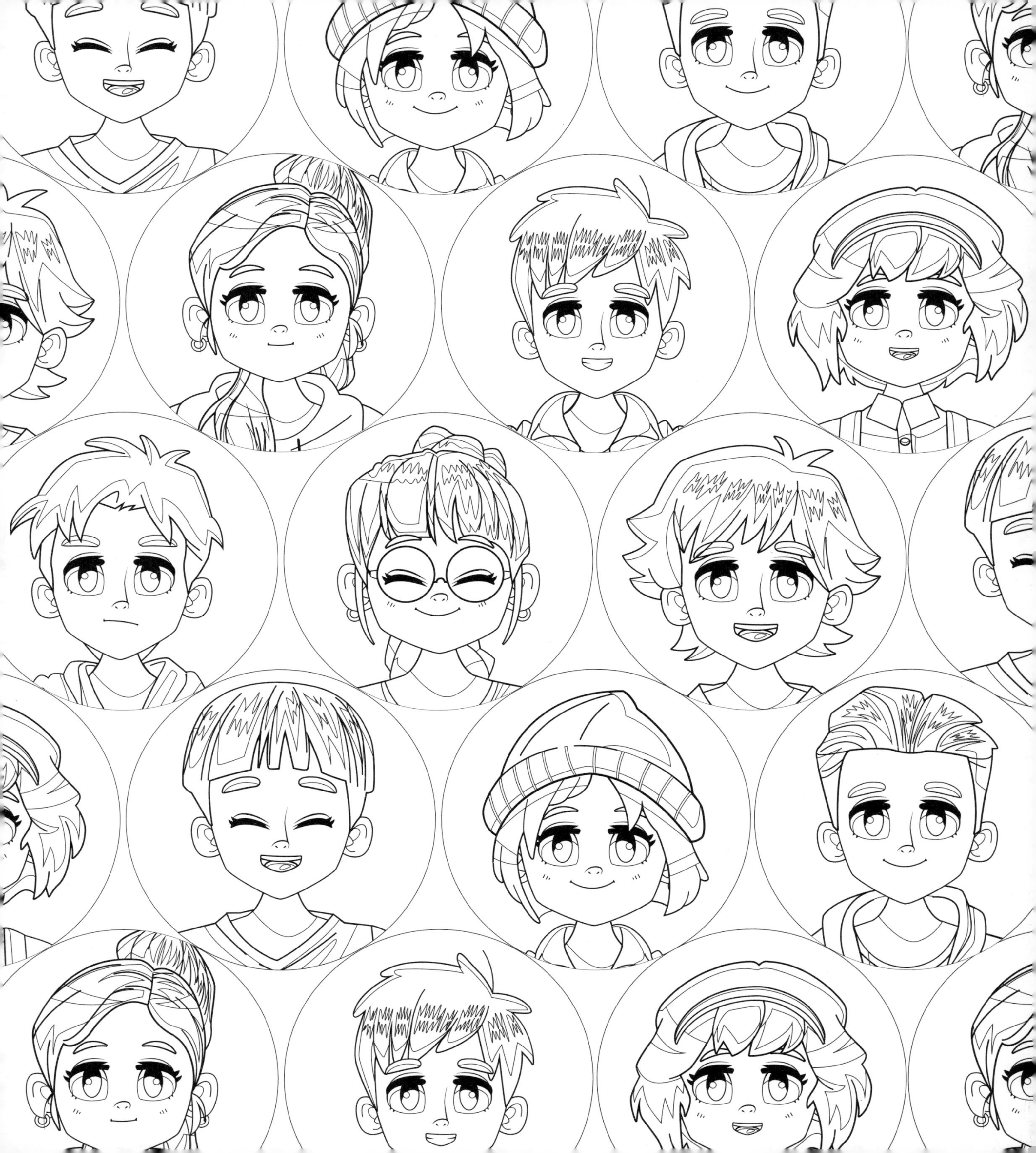

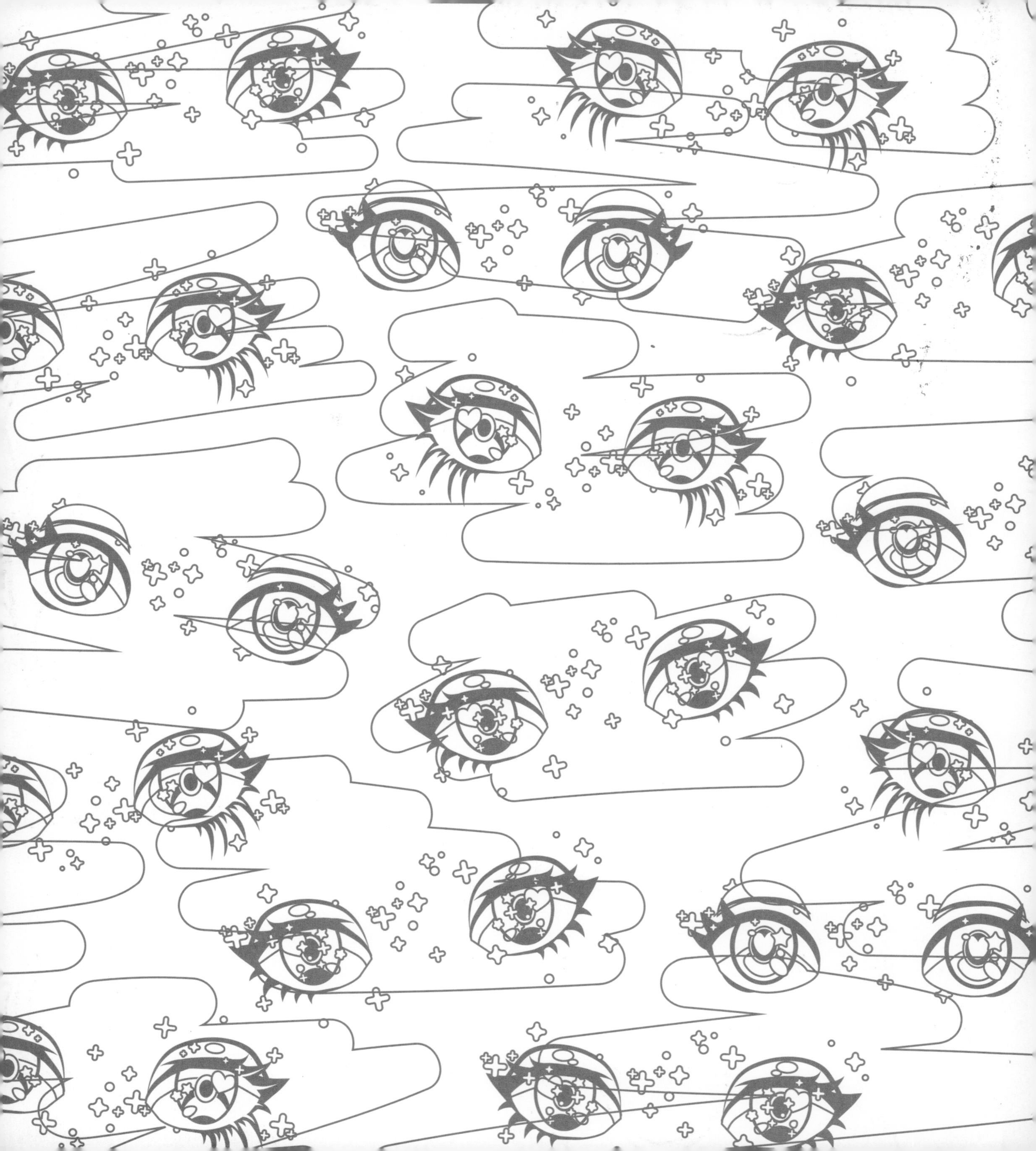

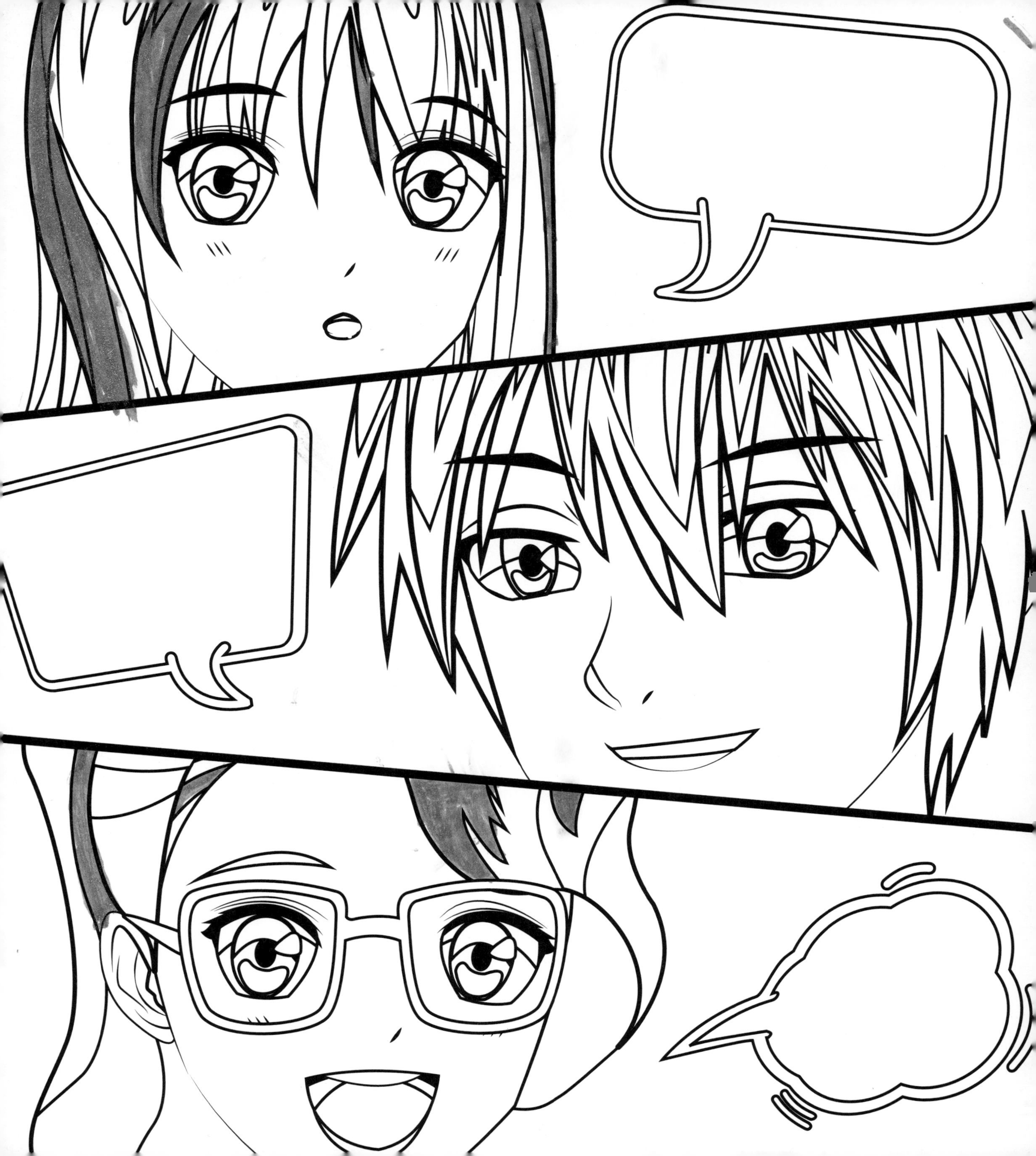

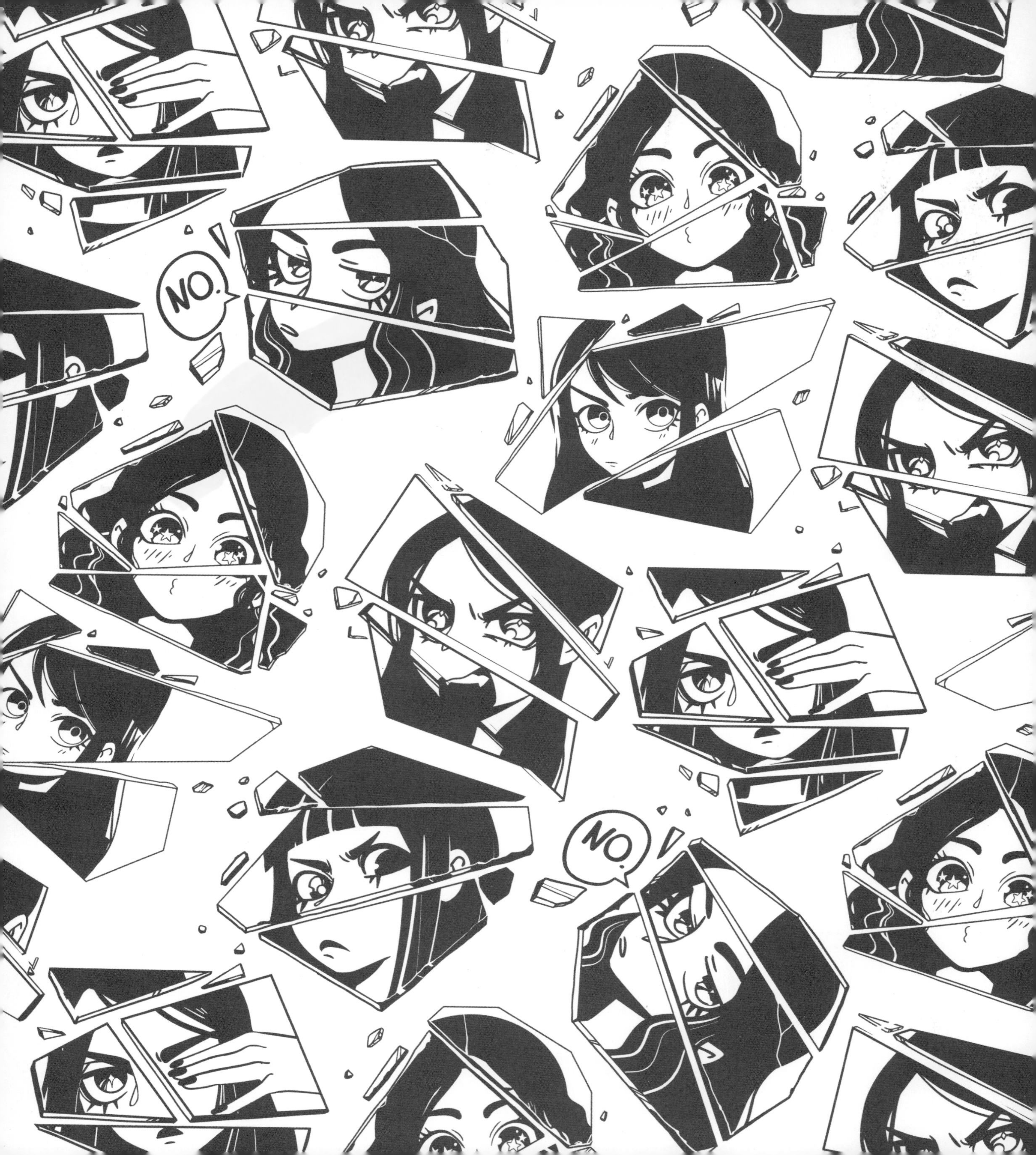
NO.
NO.

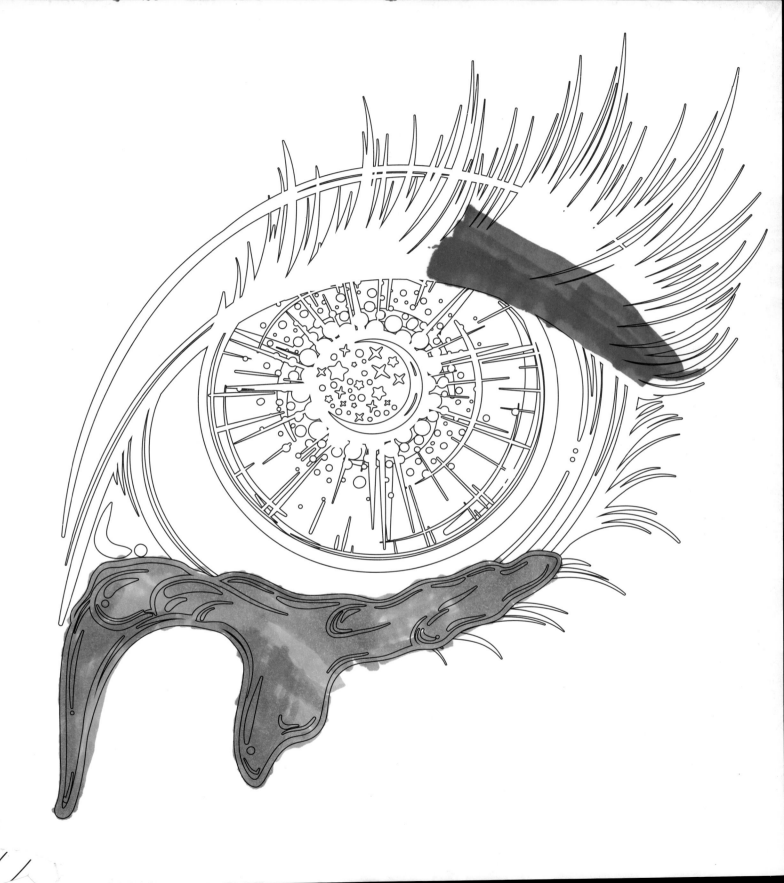

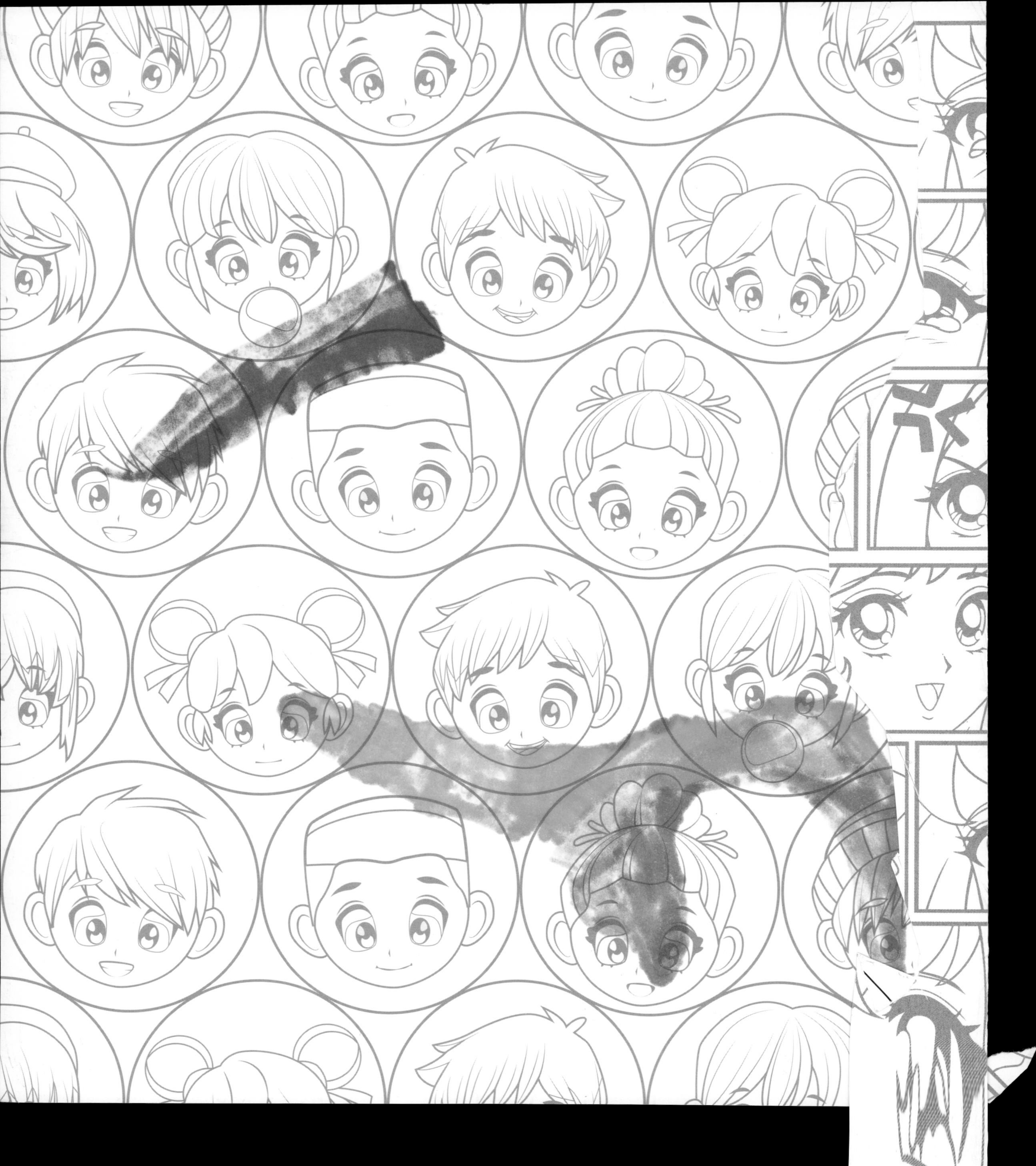

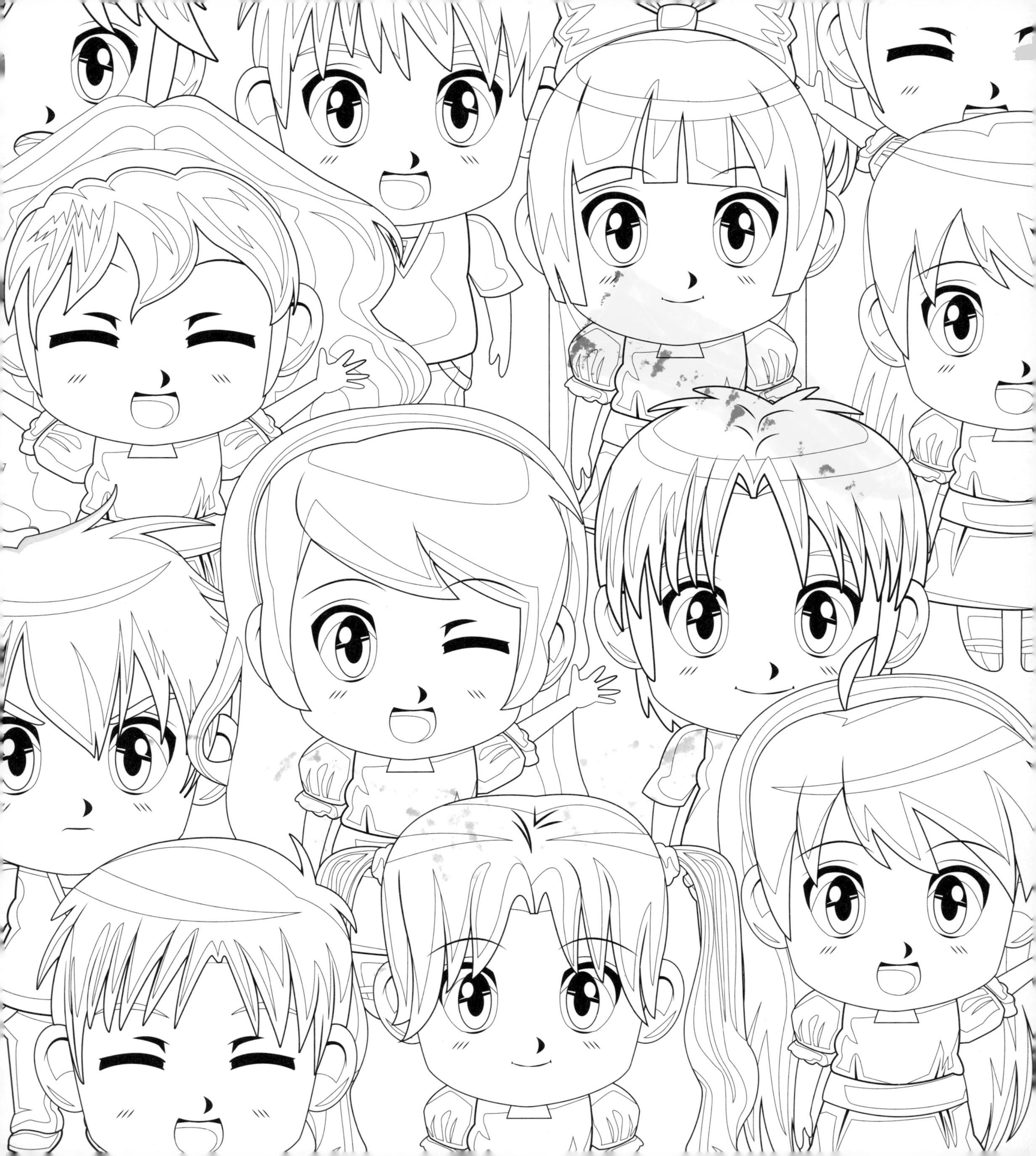

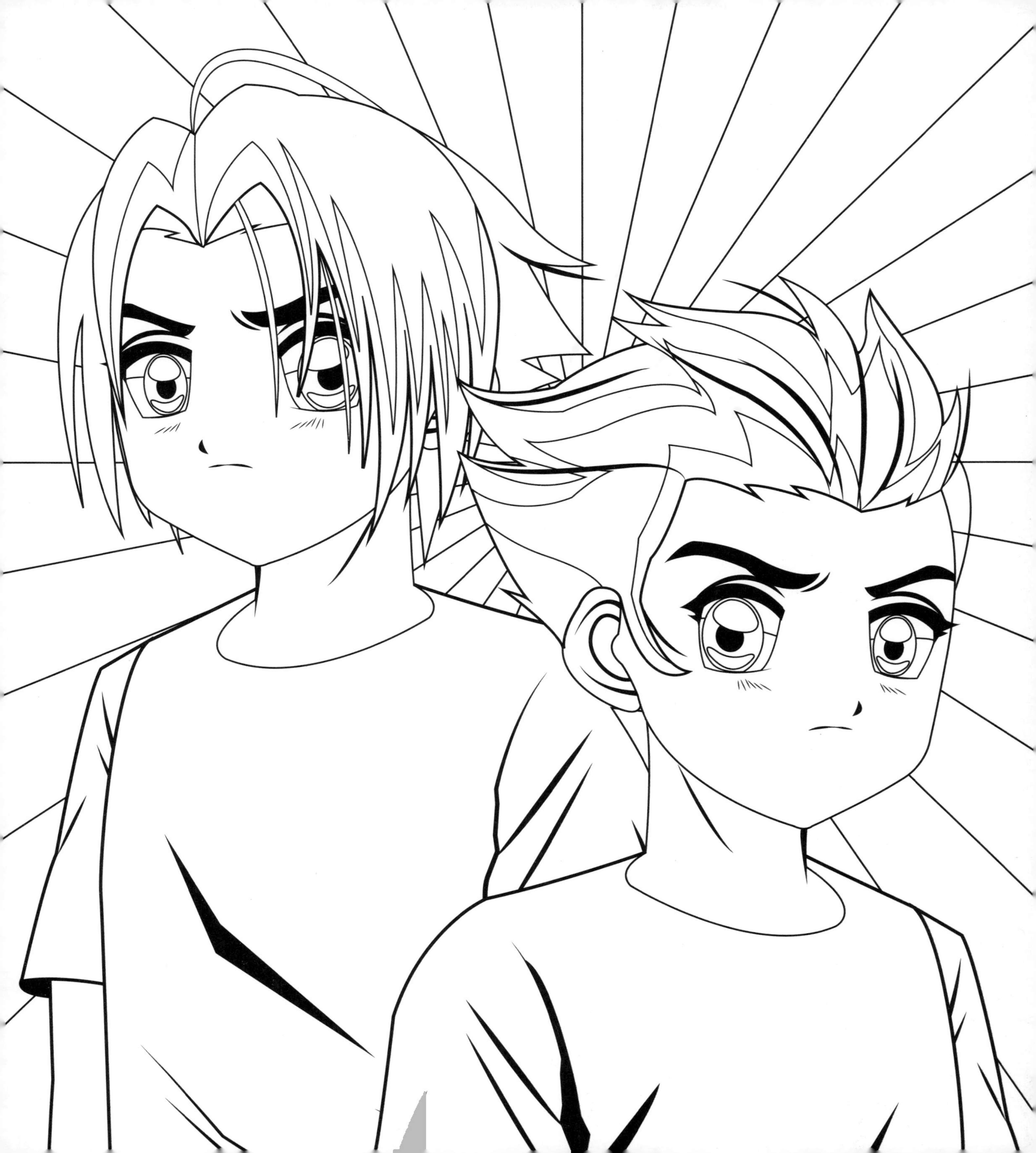

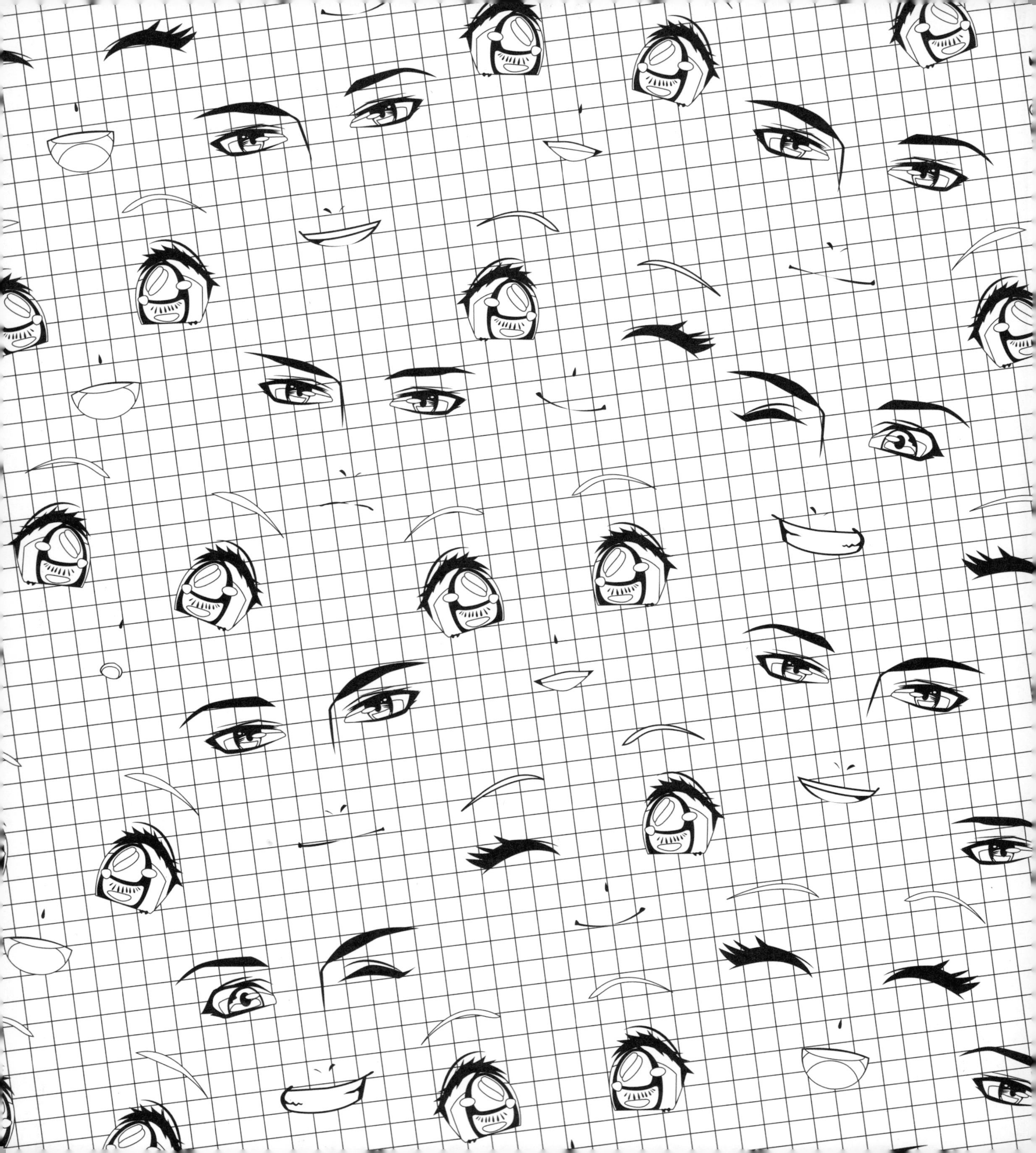

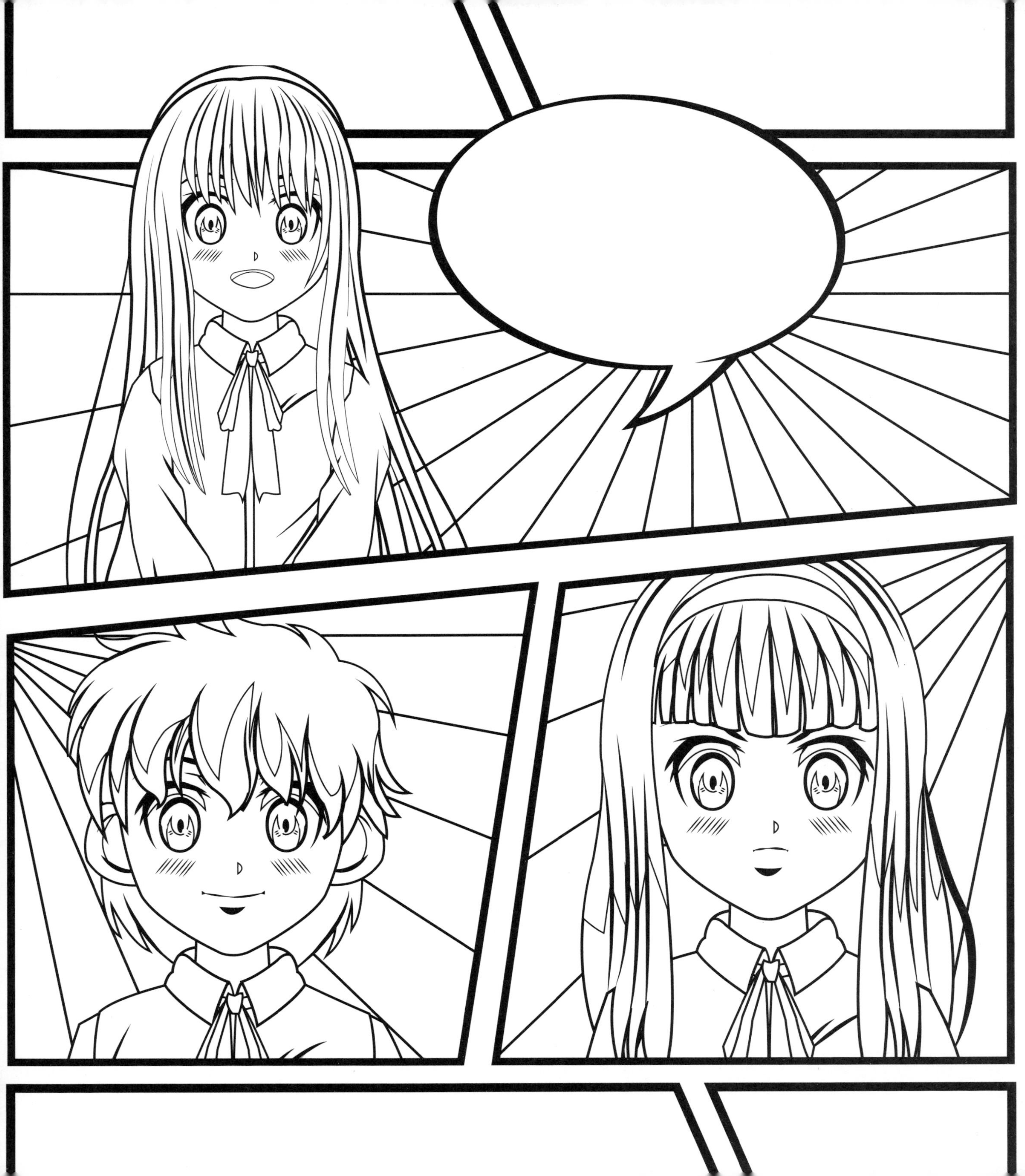

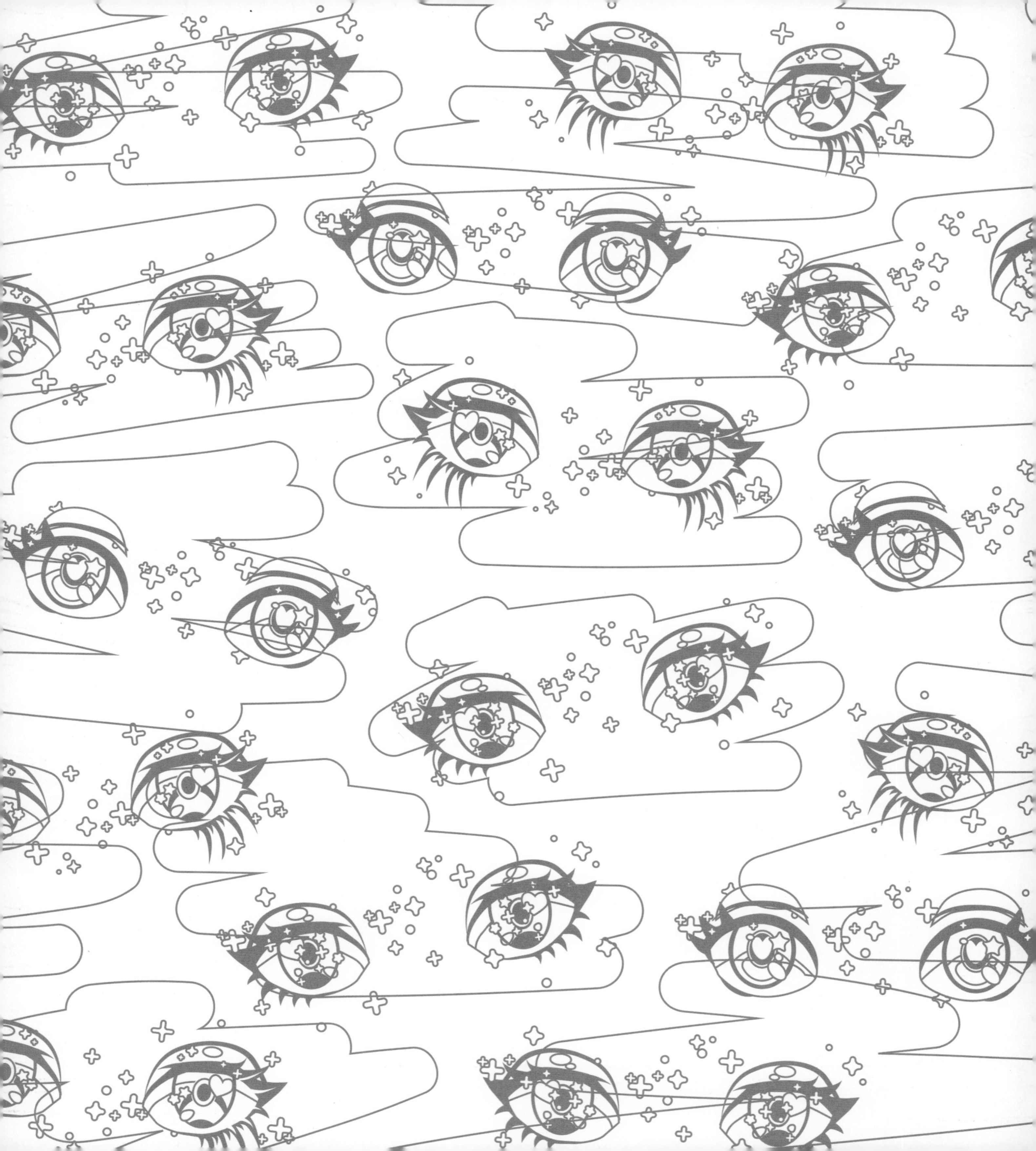

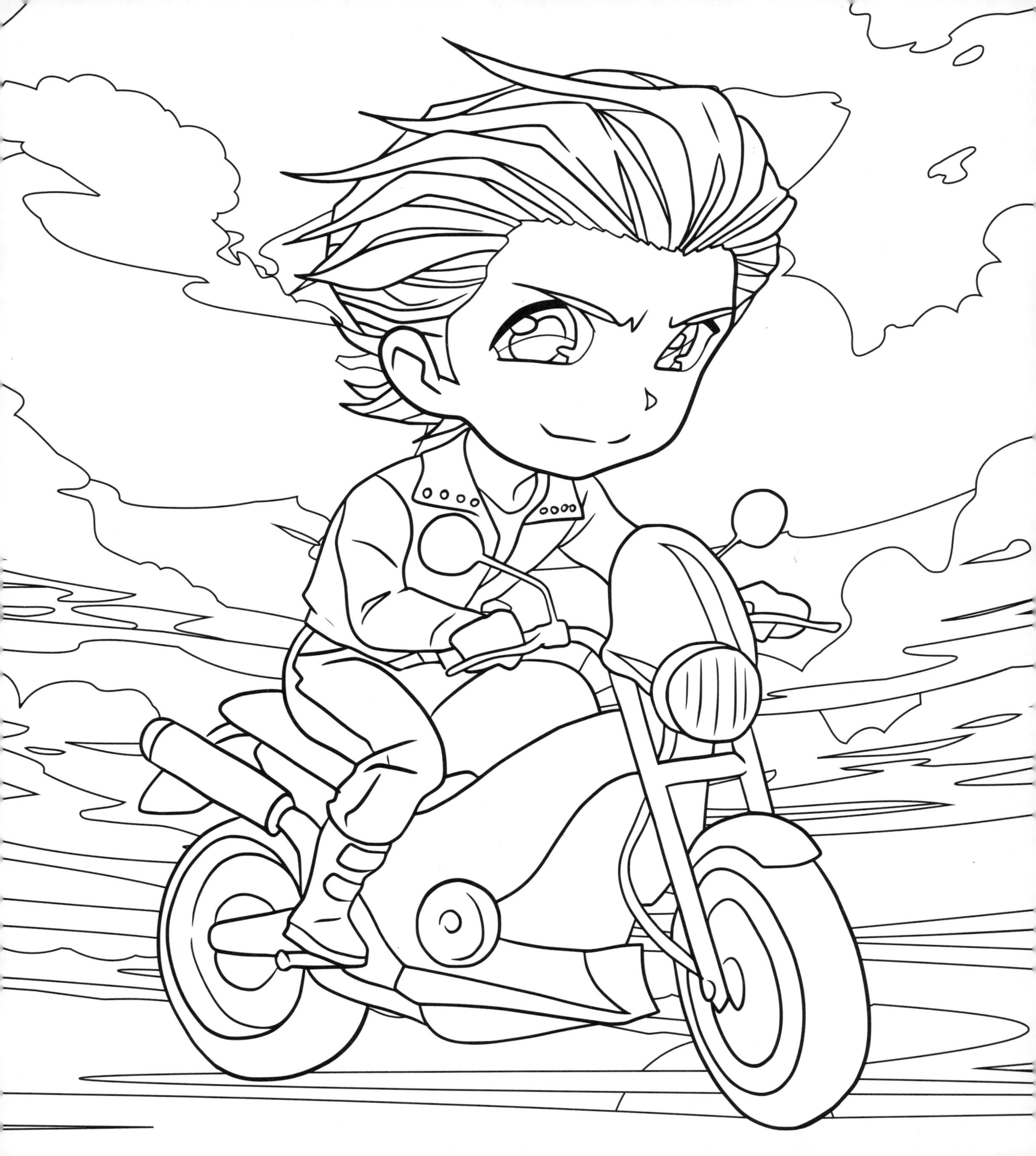

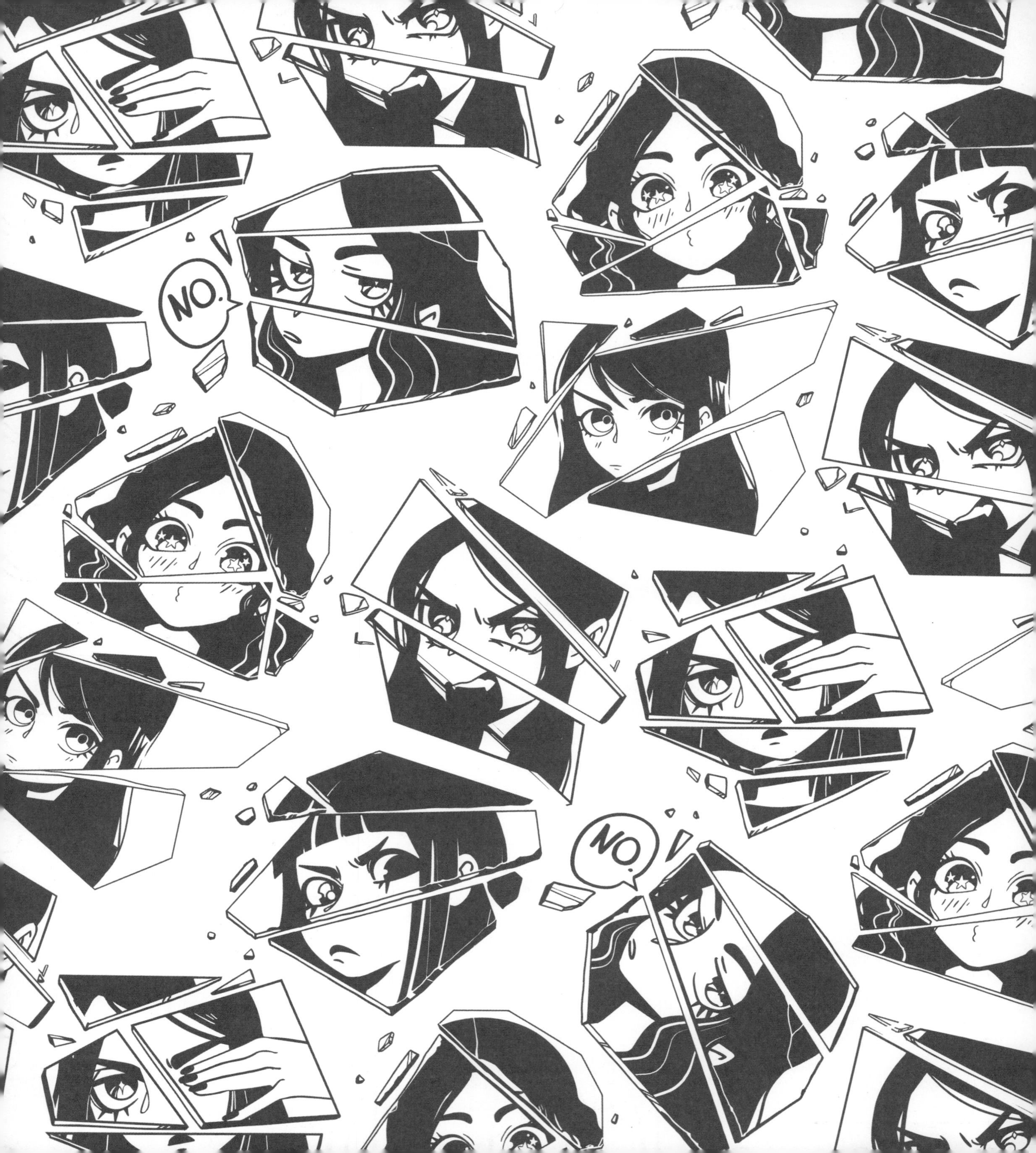
NO.
NO.

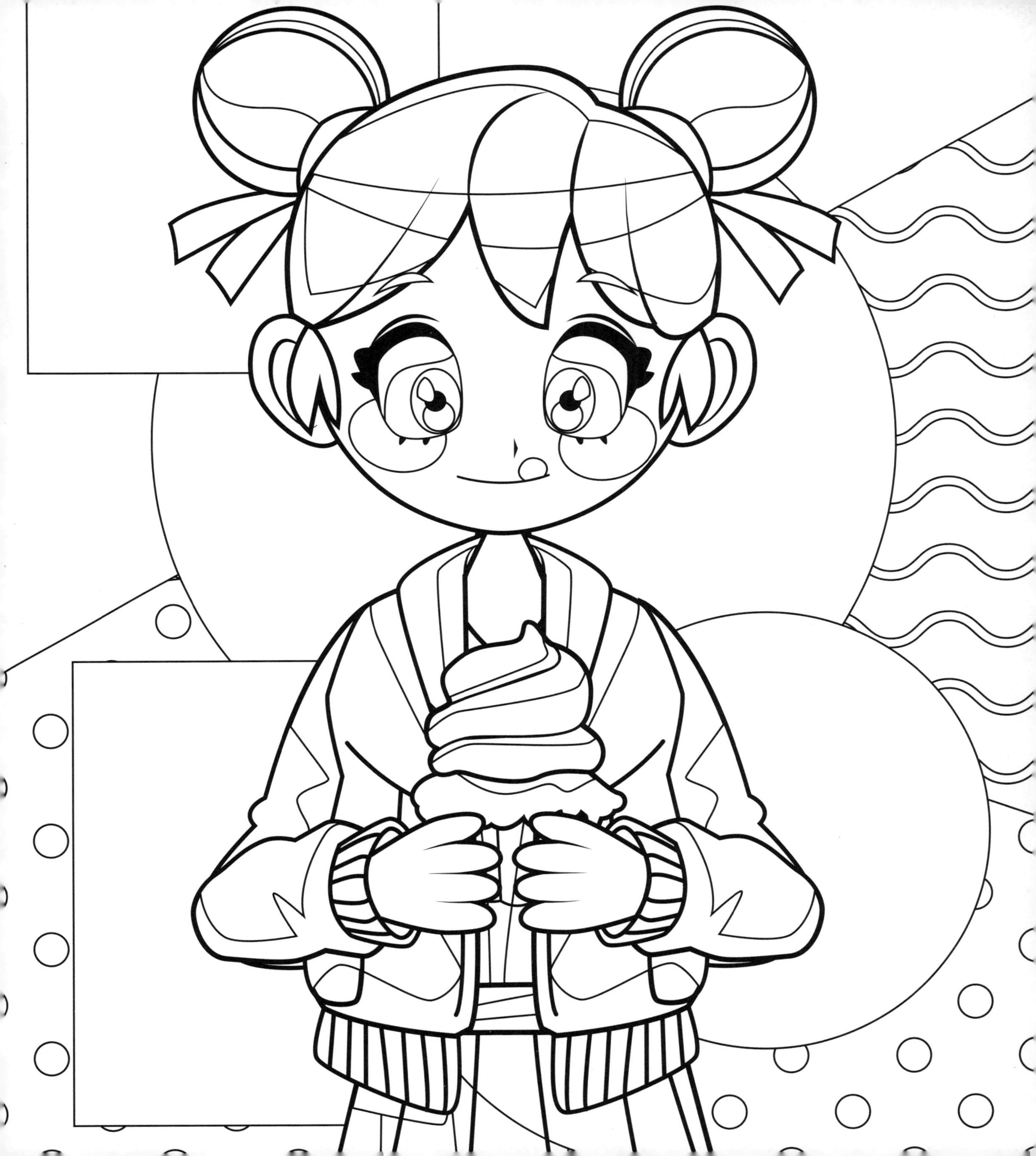

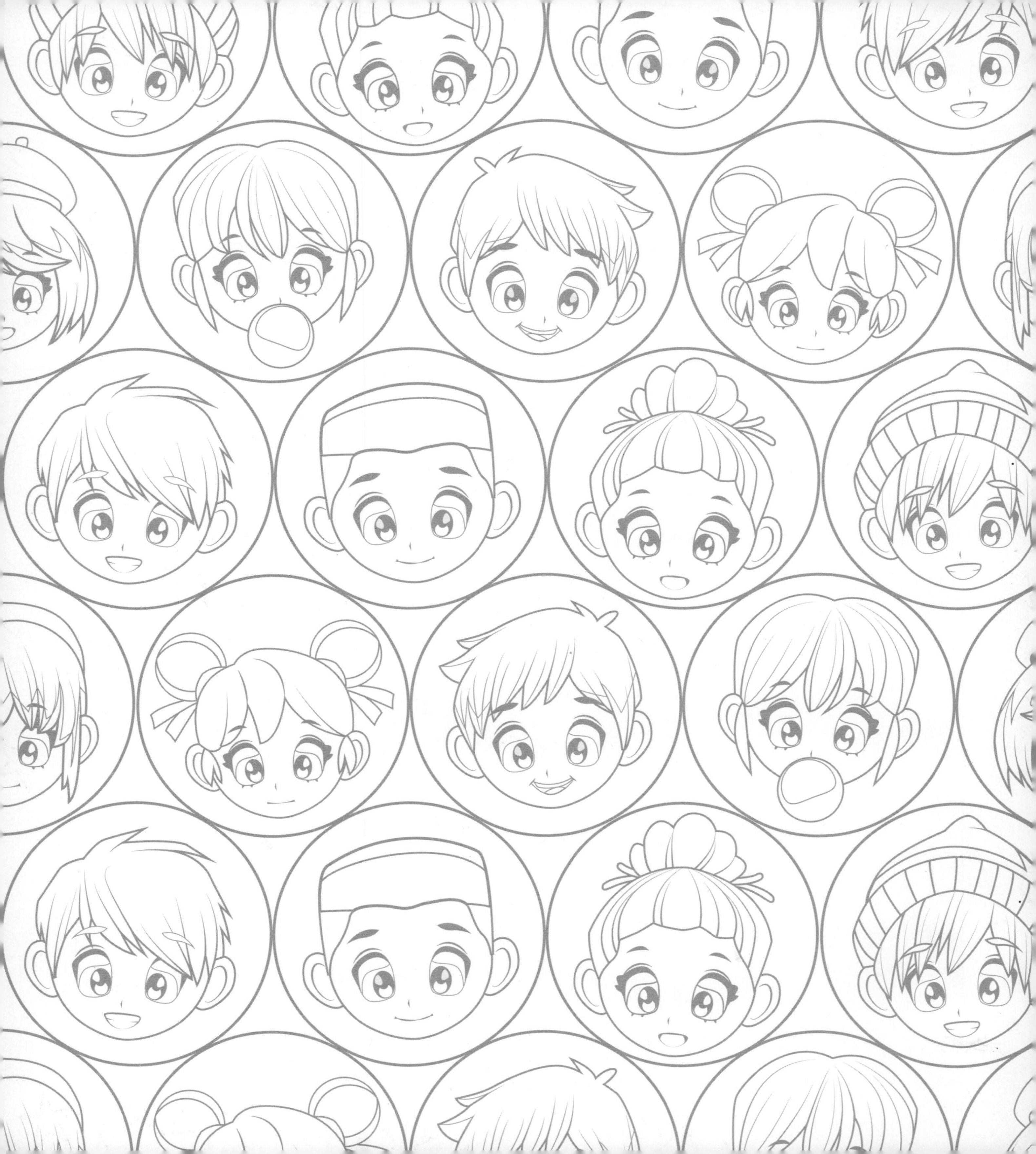

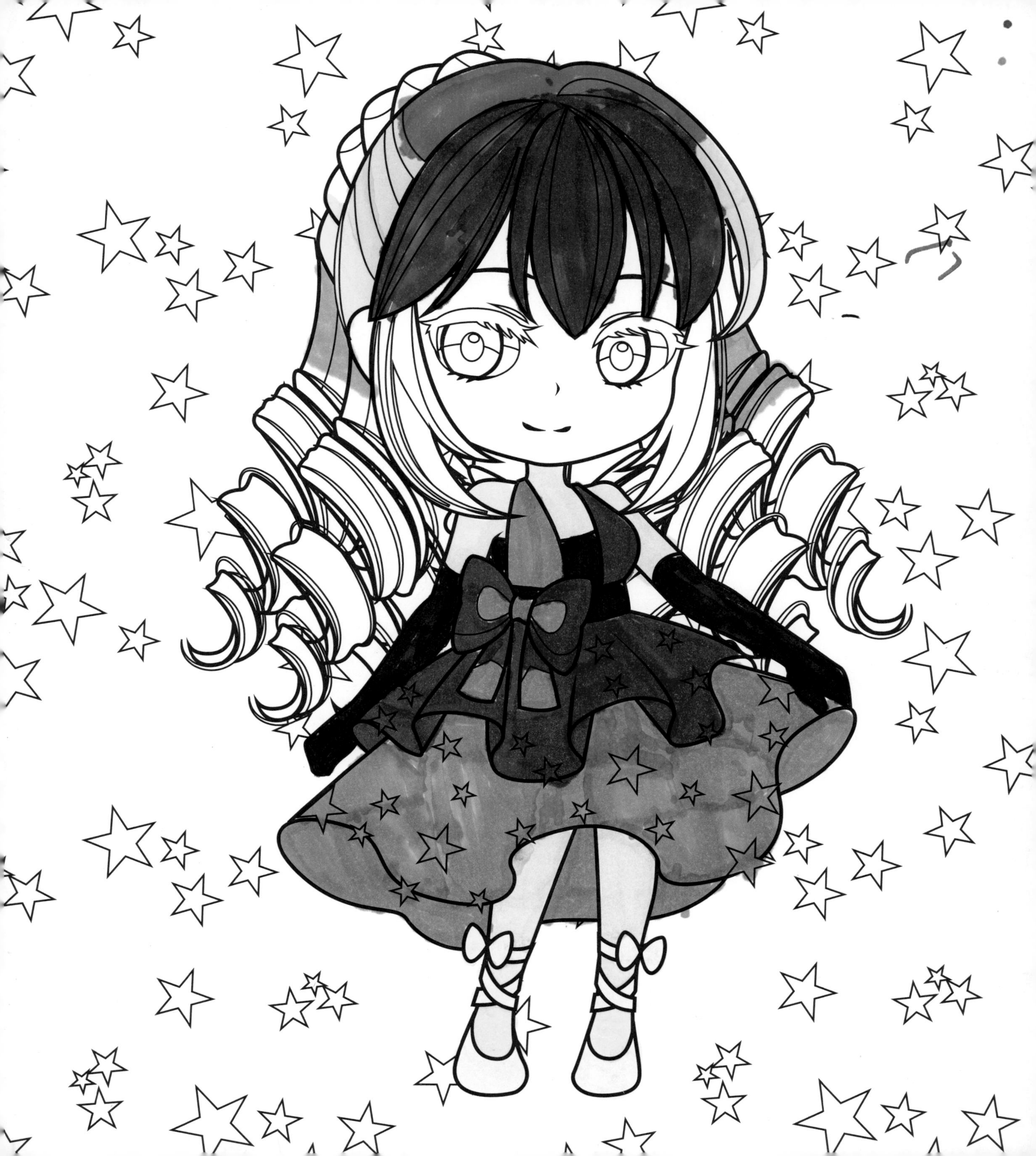

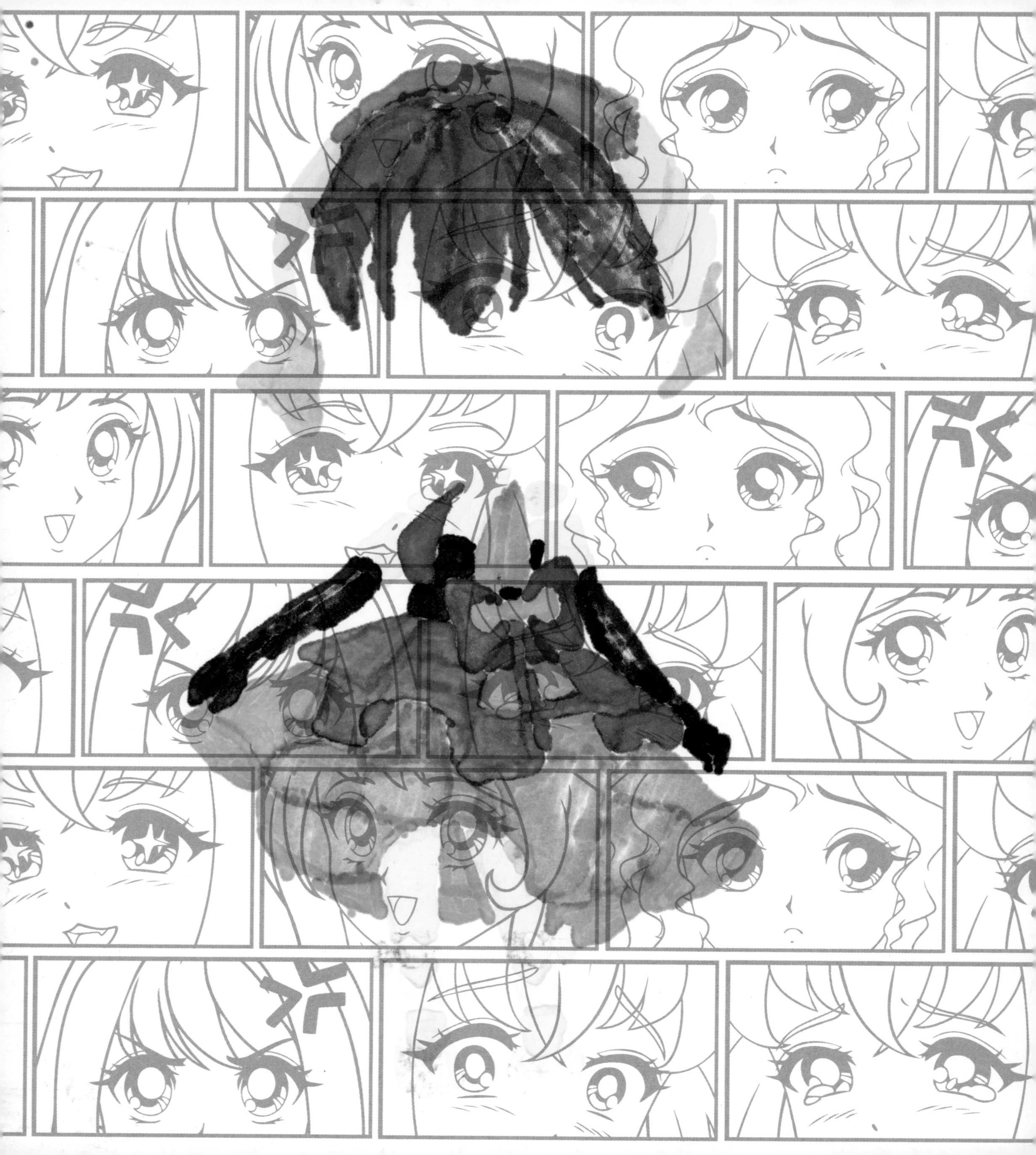

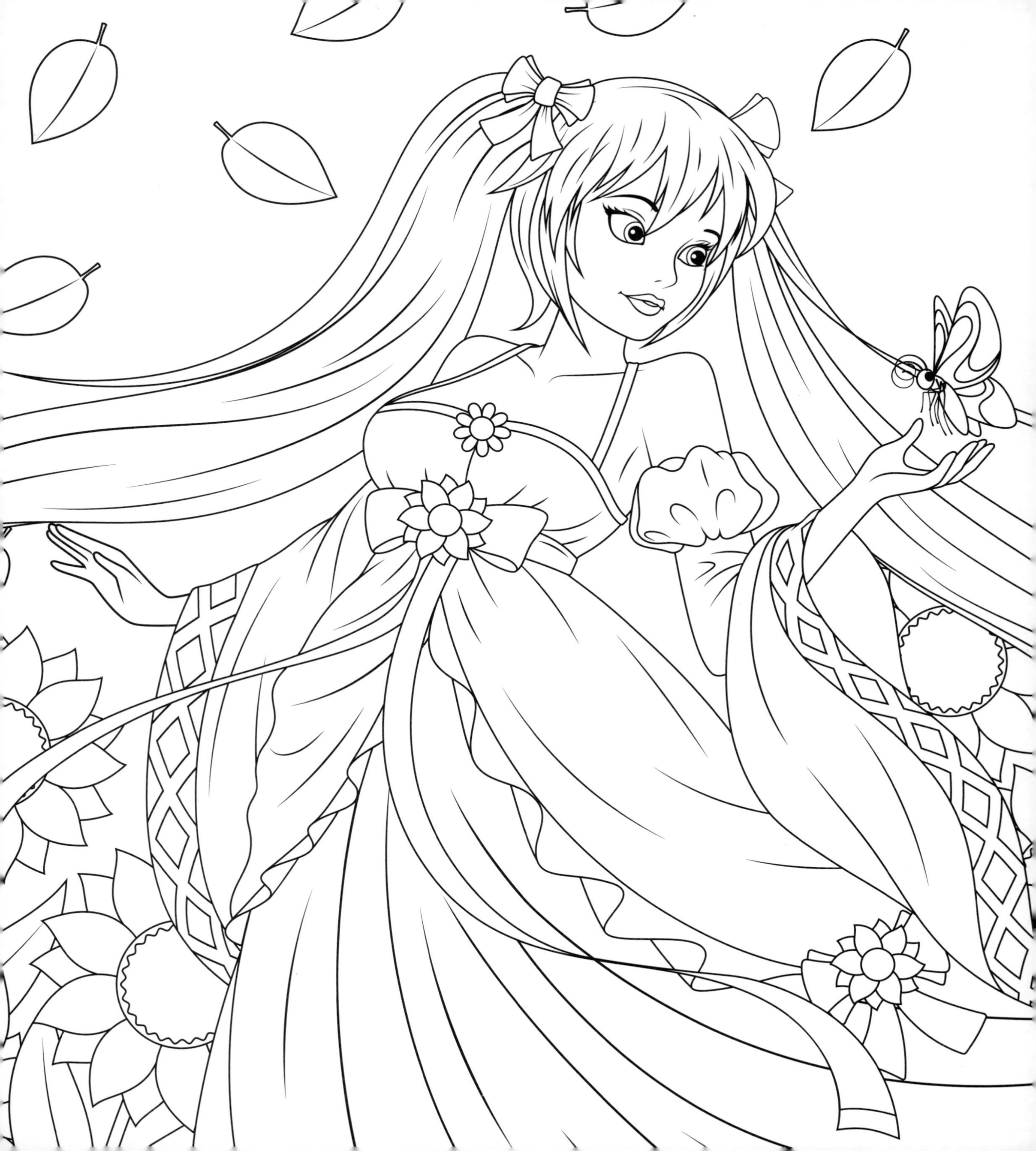

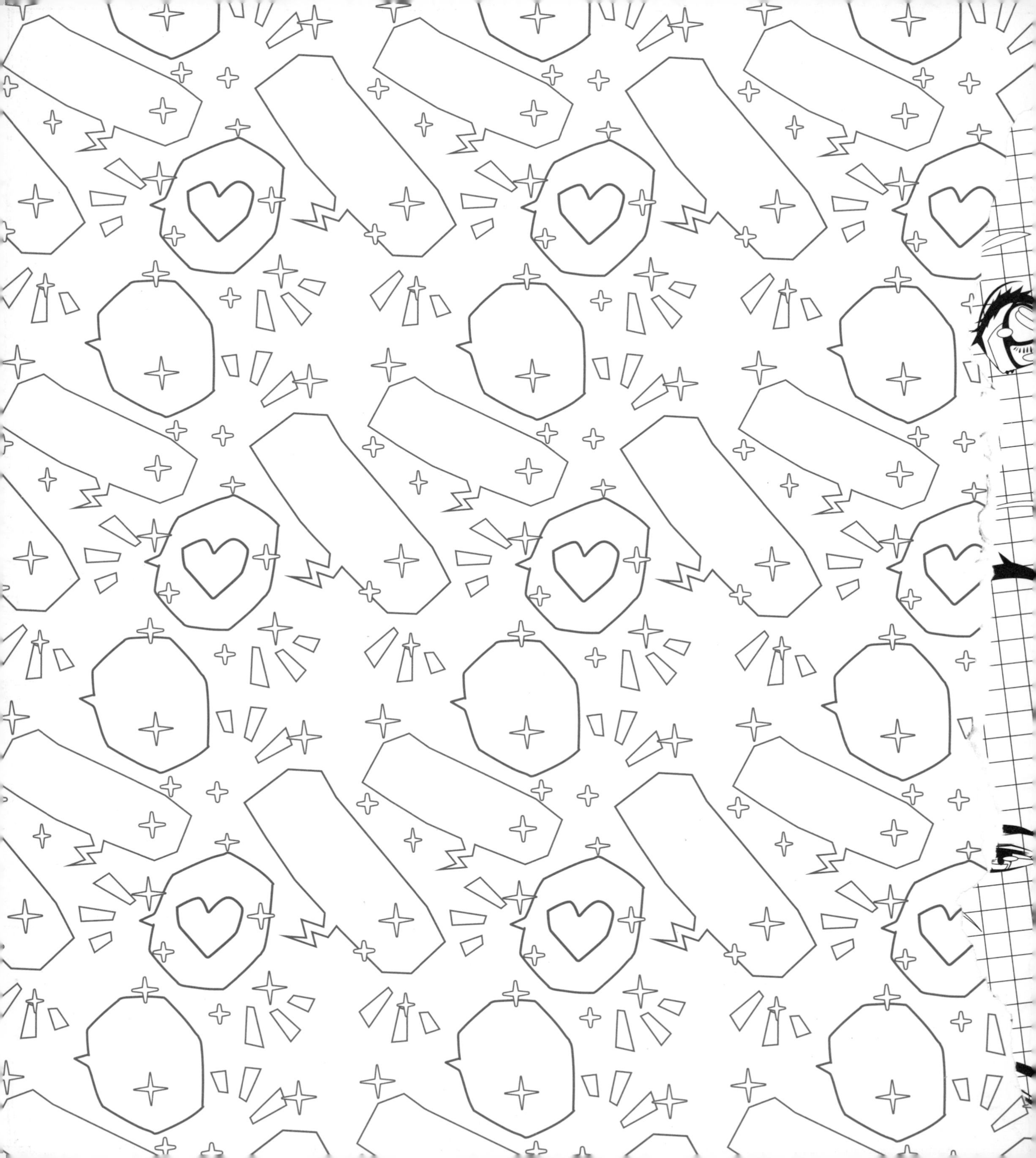

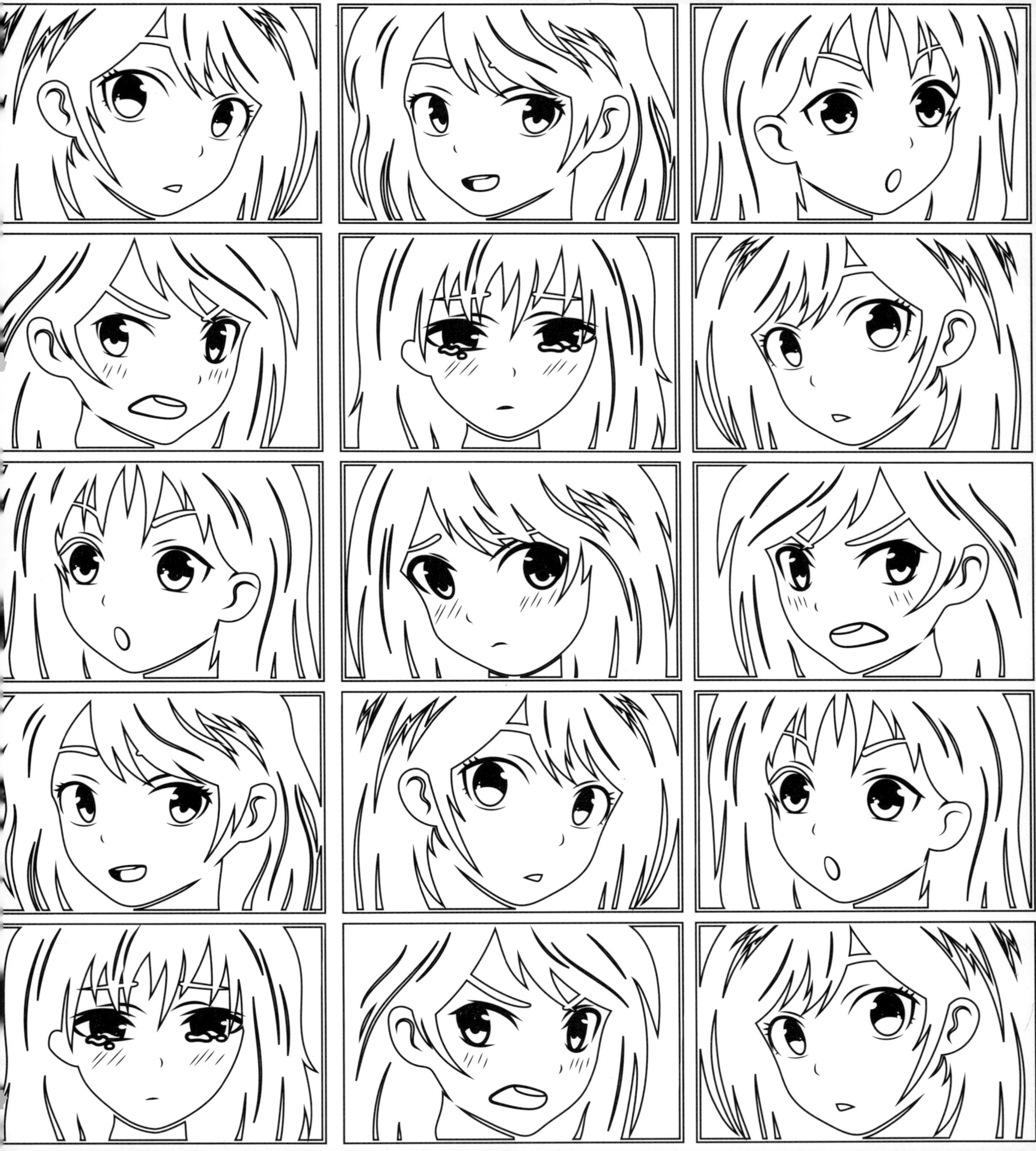

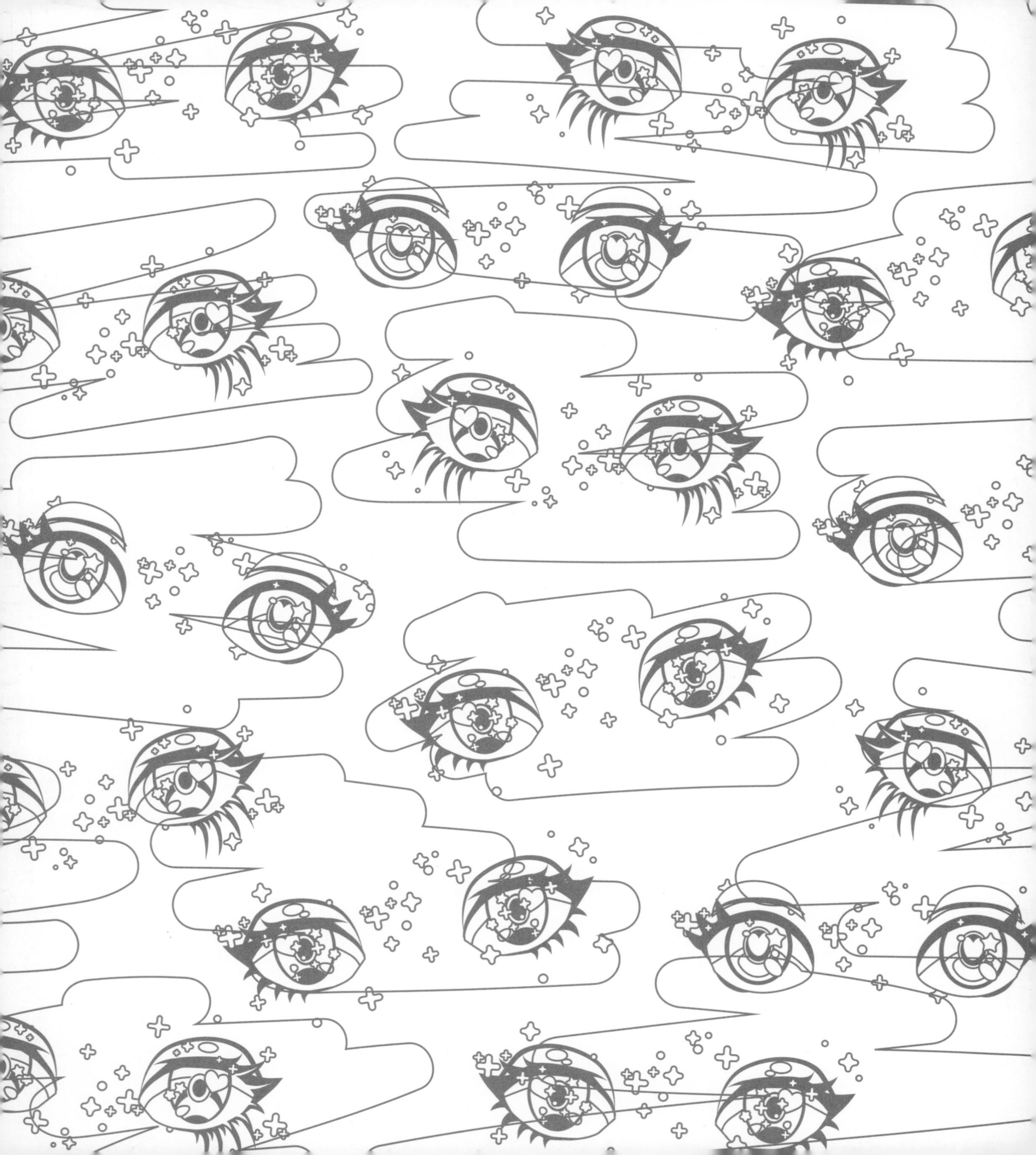

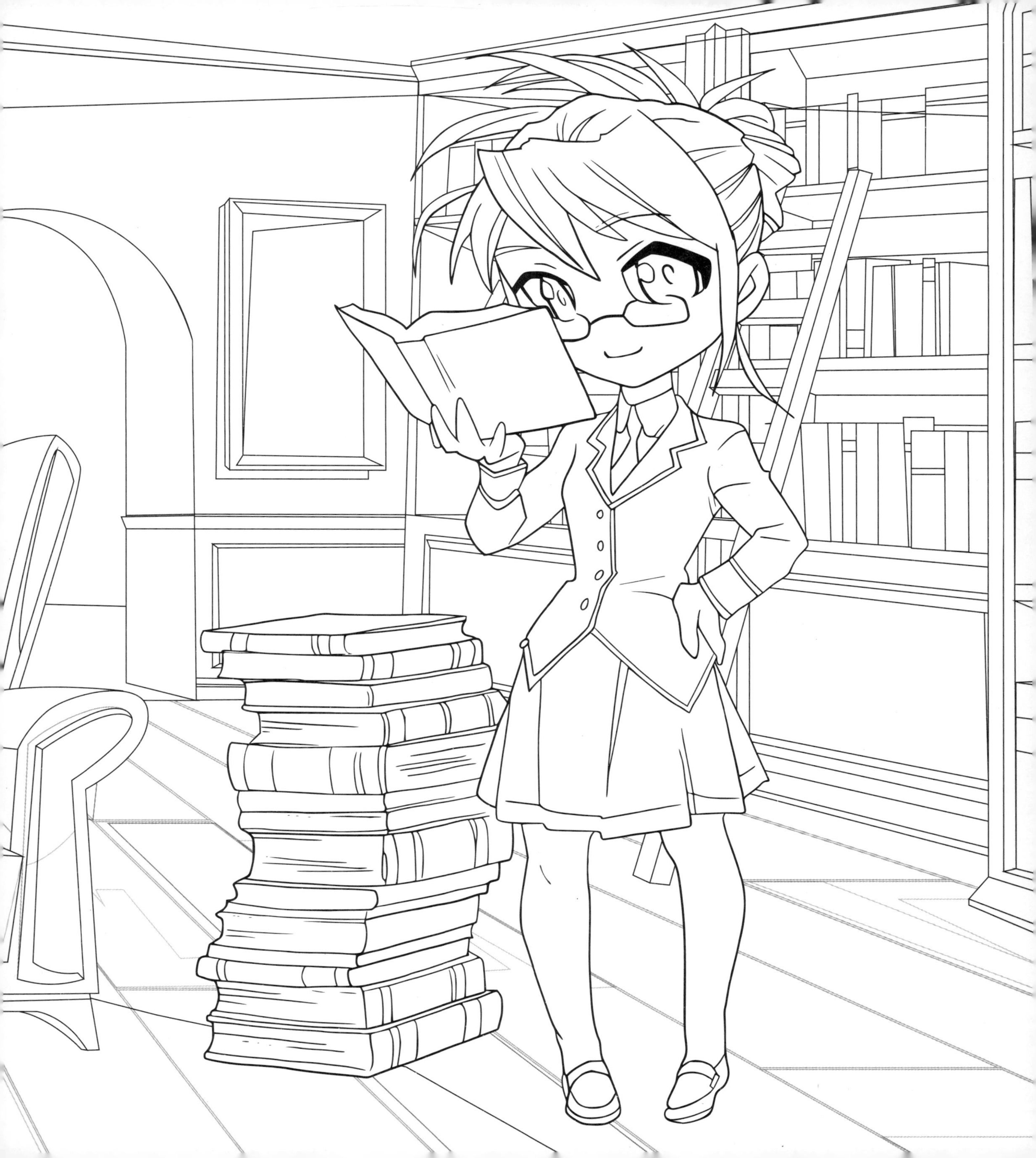

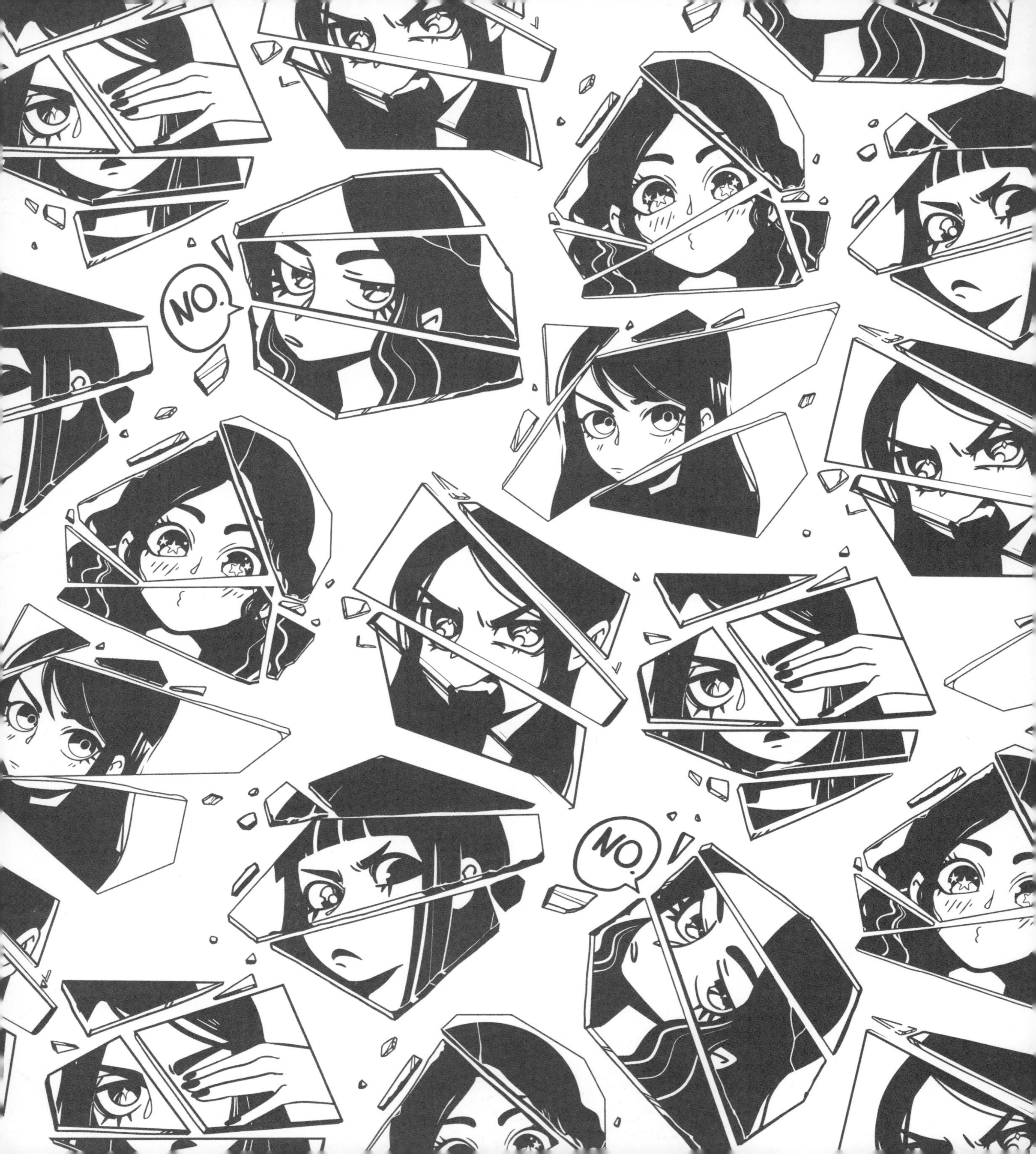
NO.
NO.

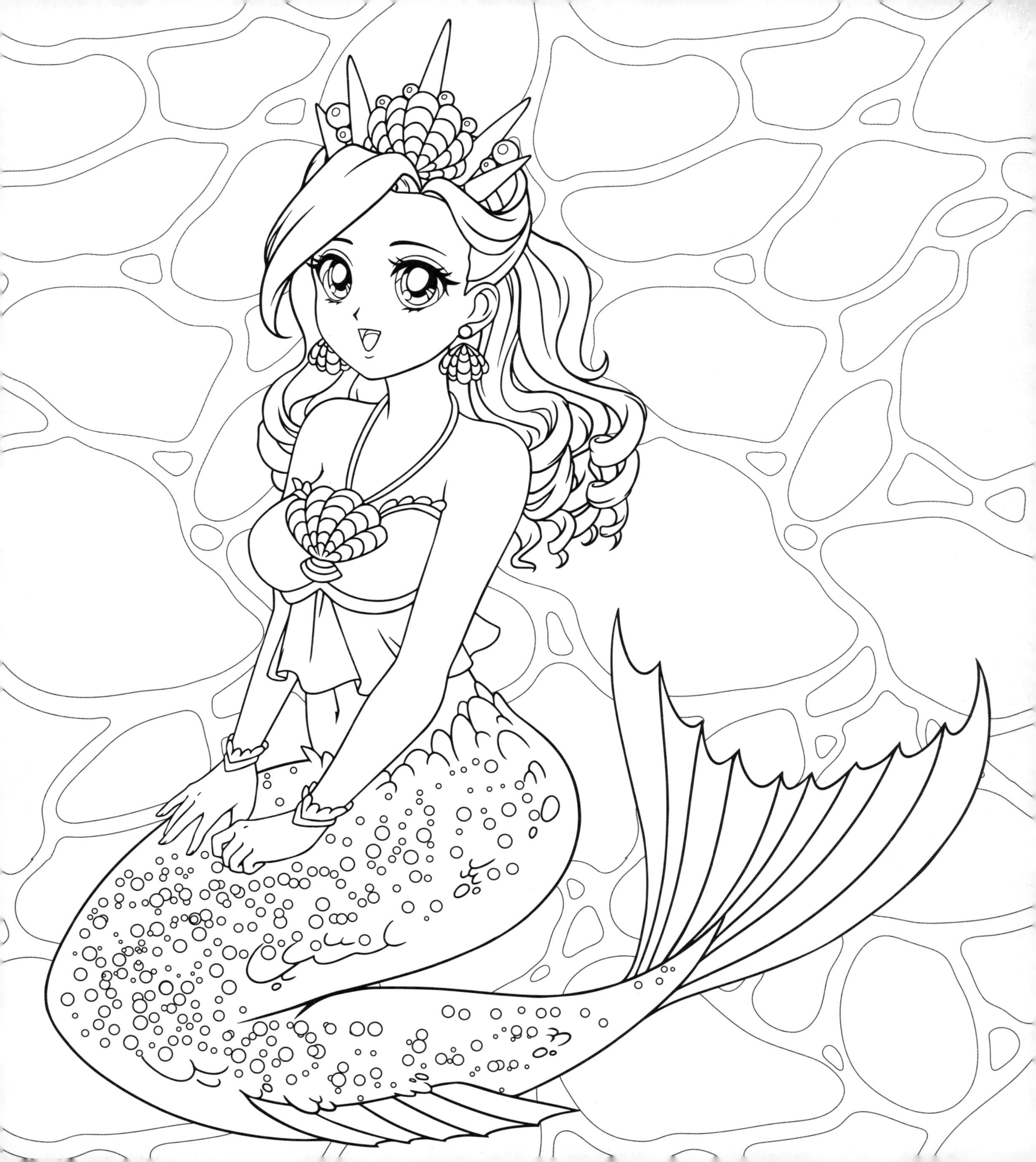

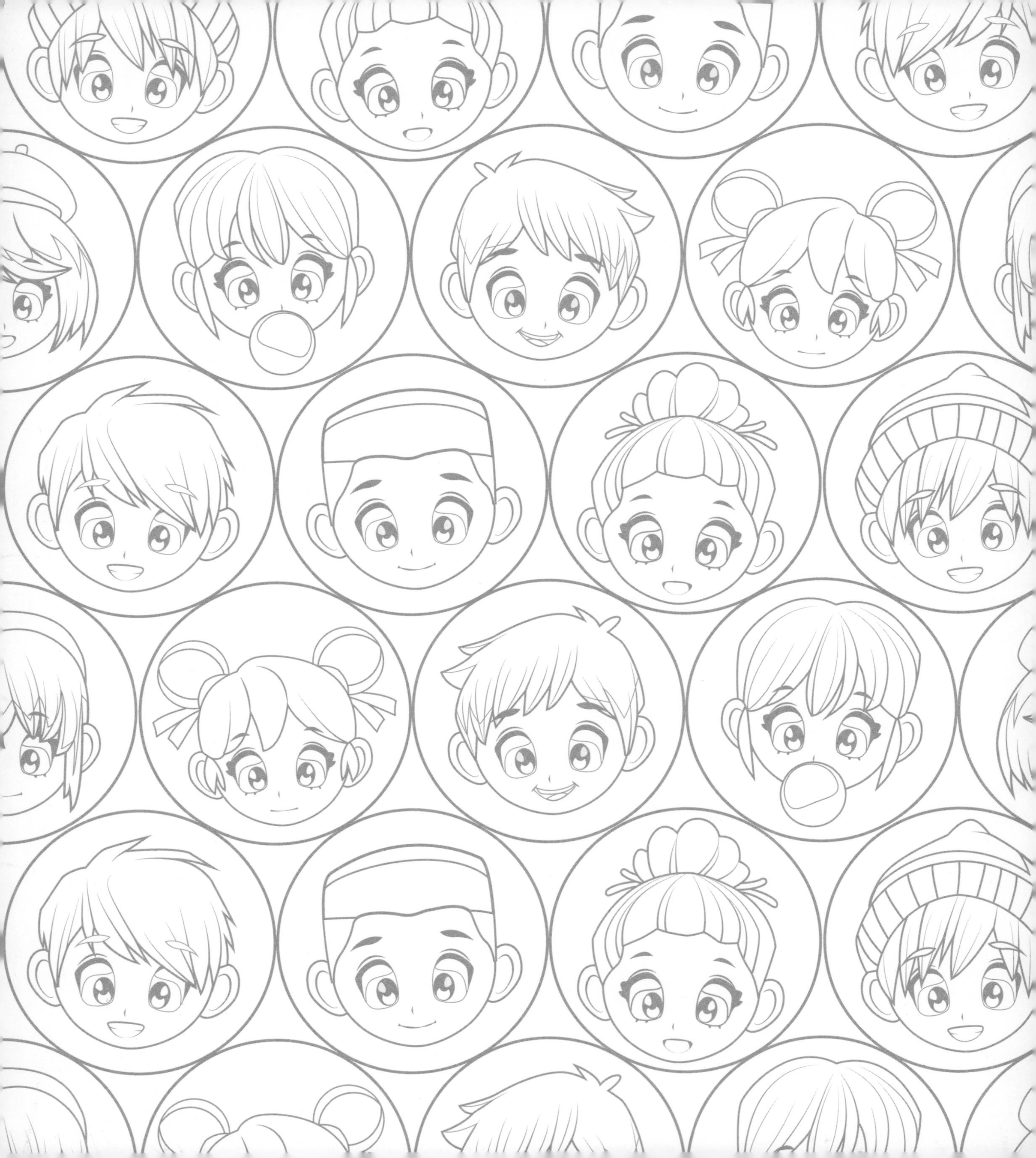

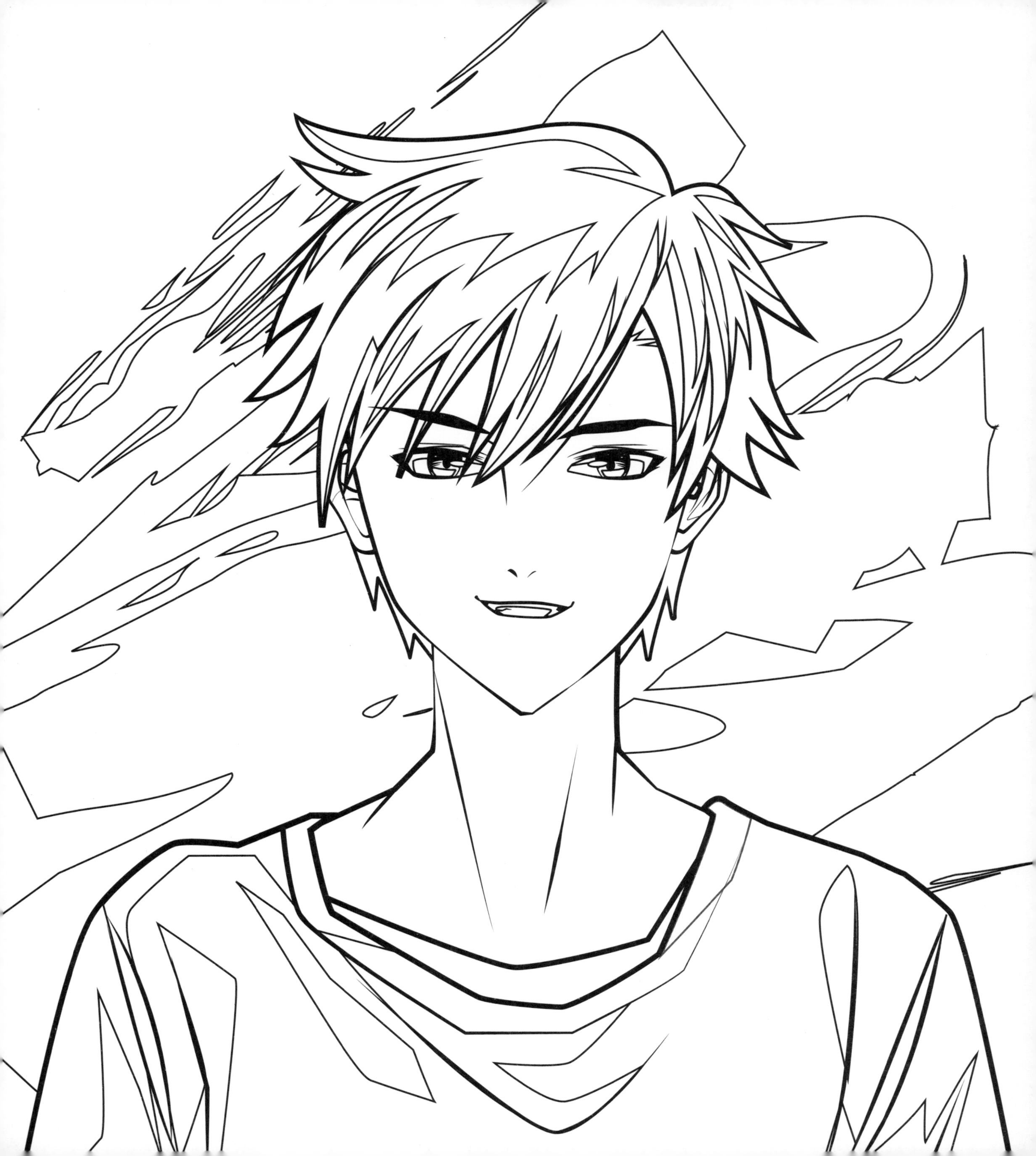

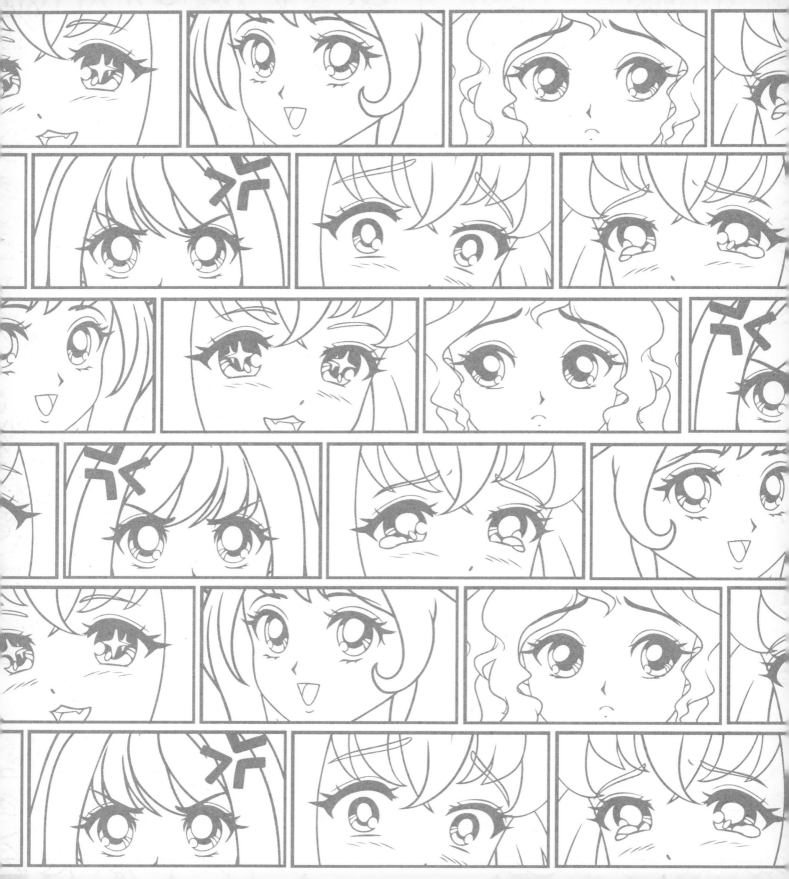

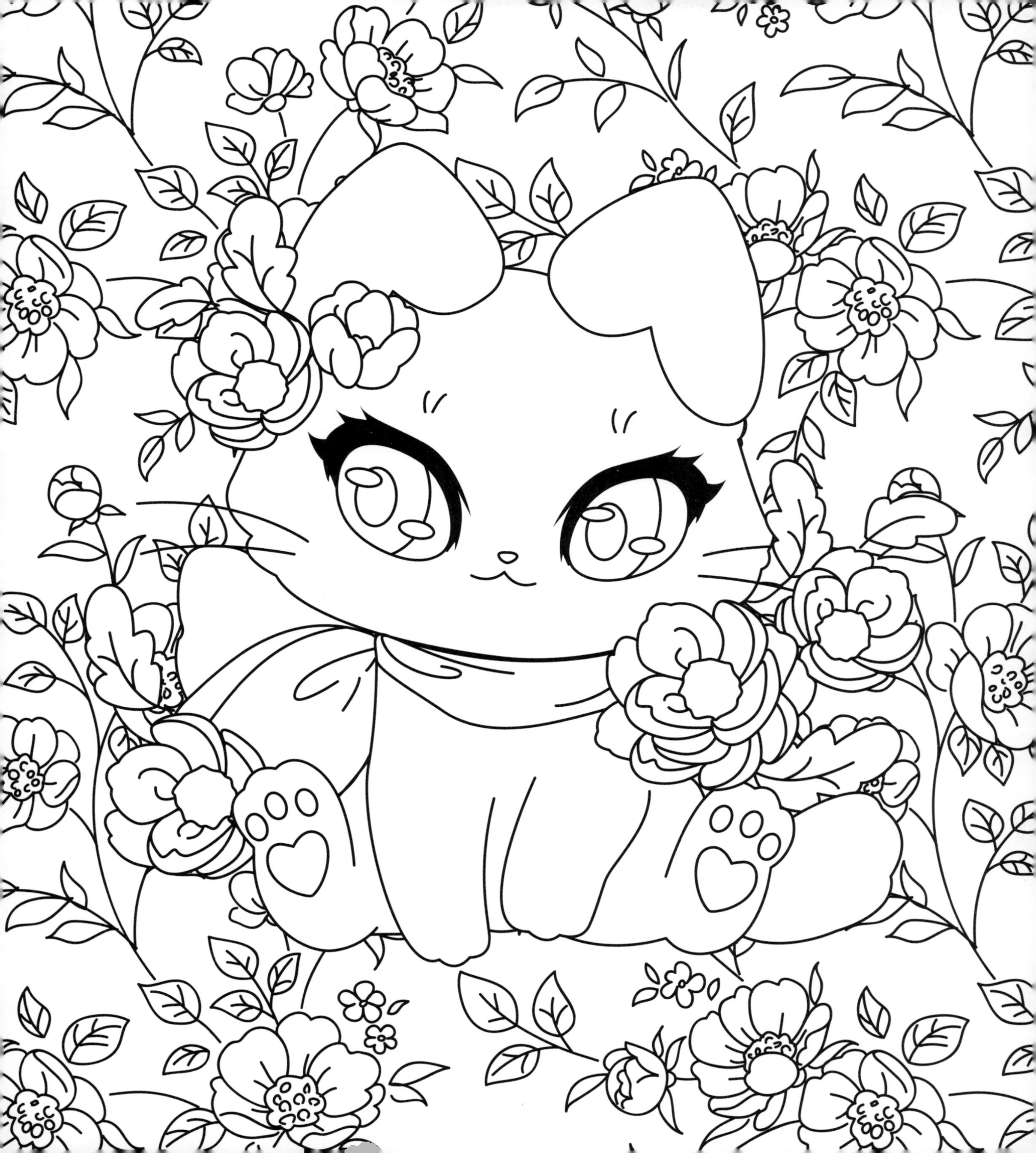

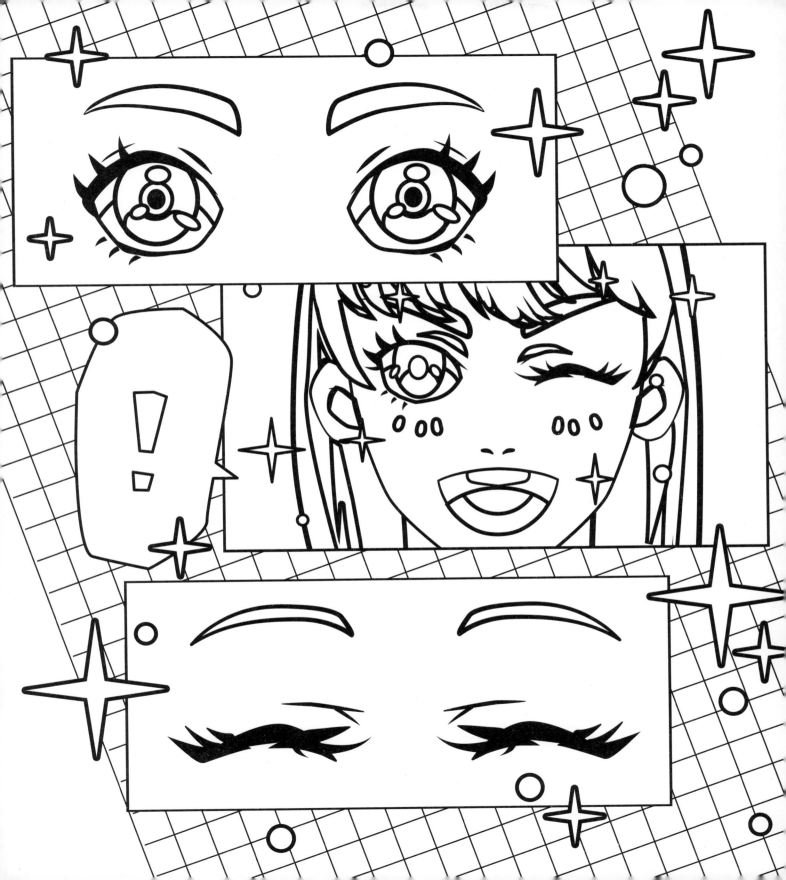

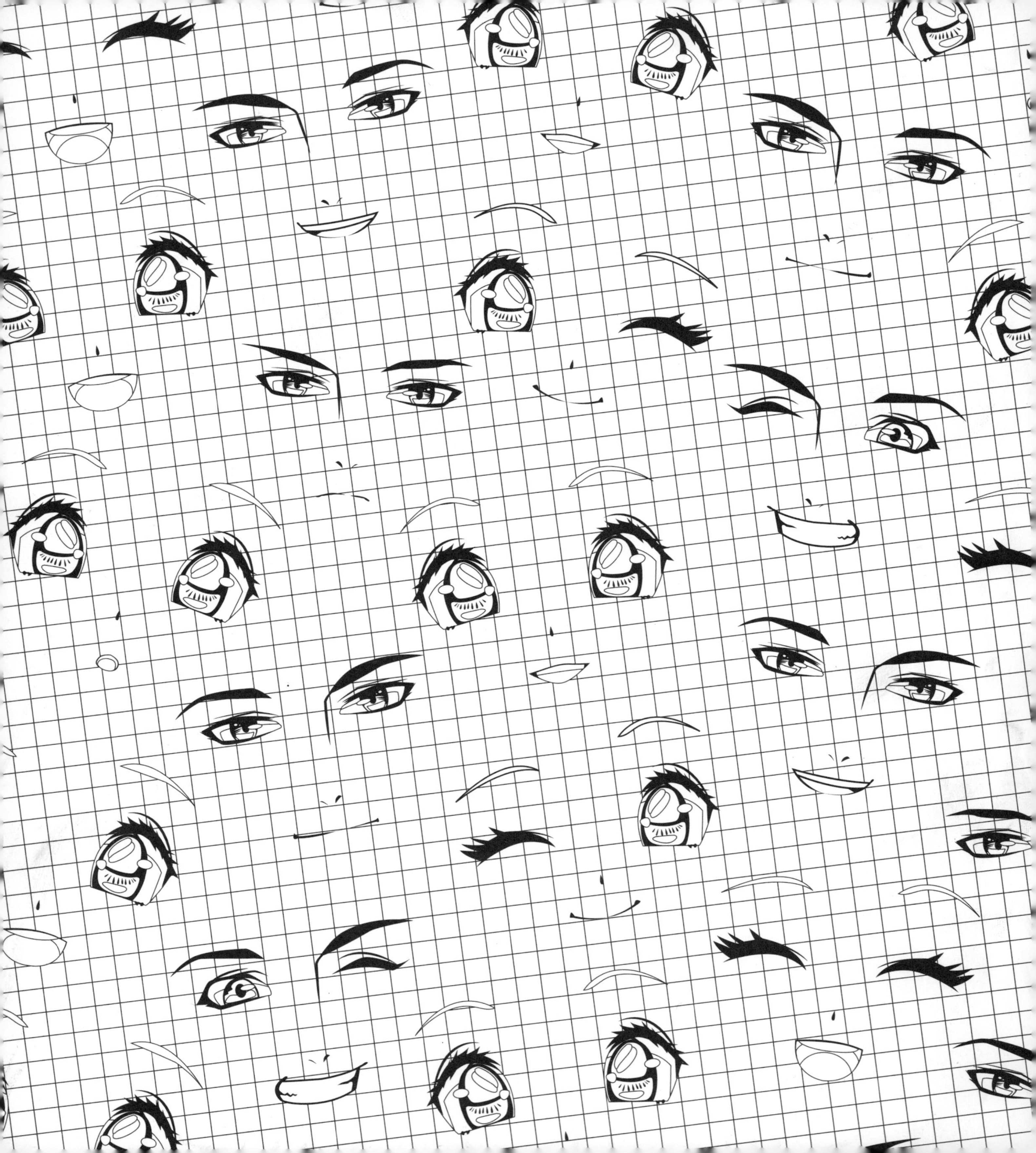

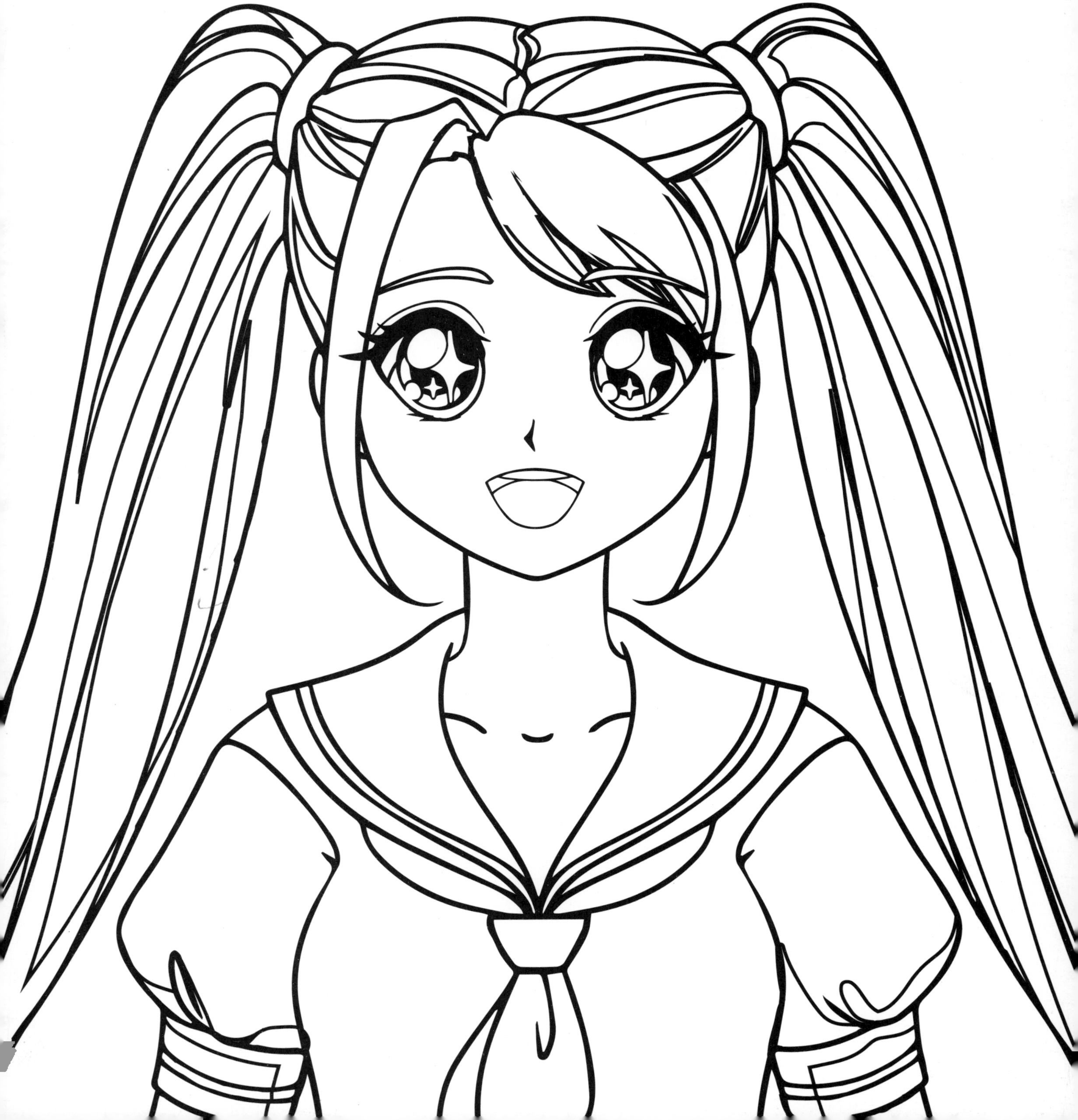

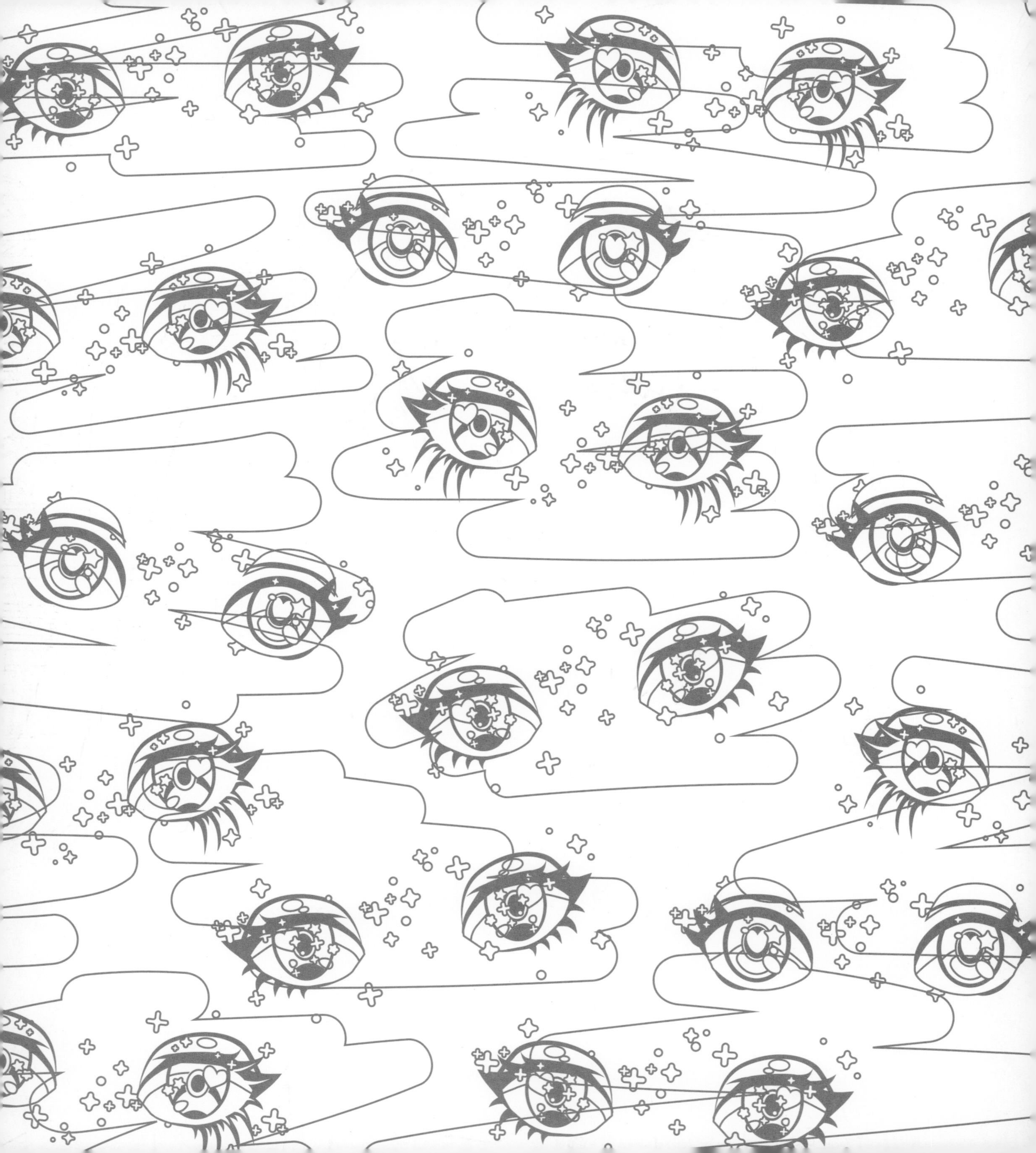

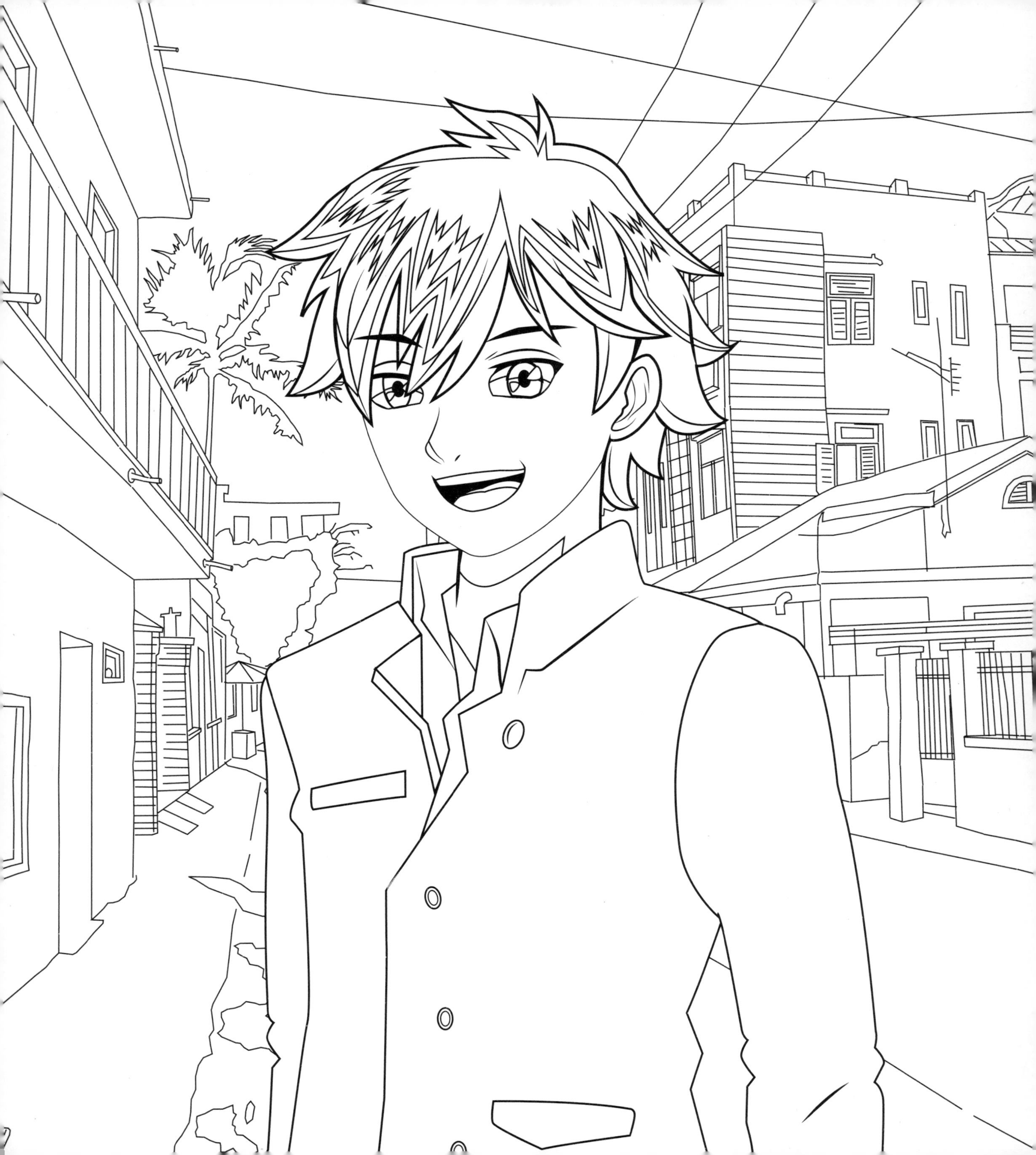

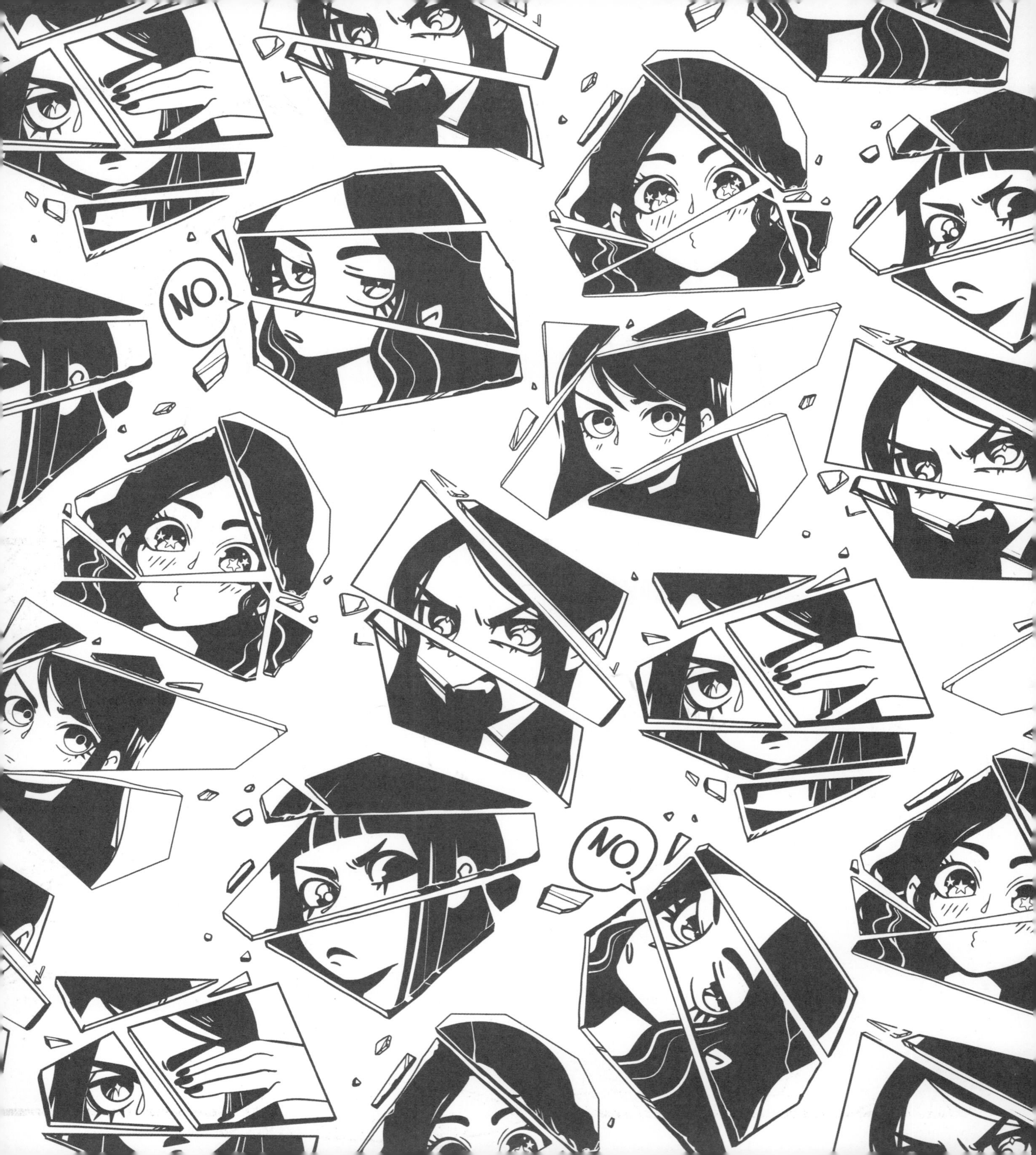
NO.
NO.

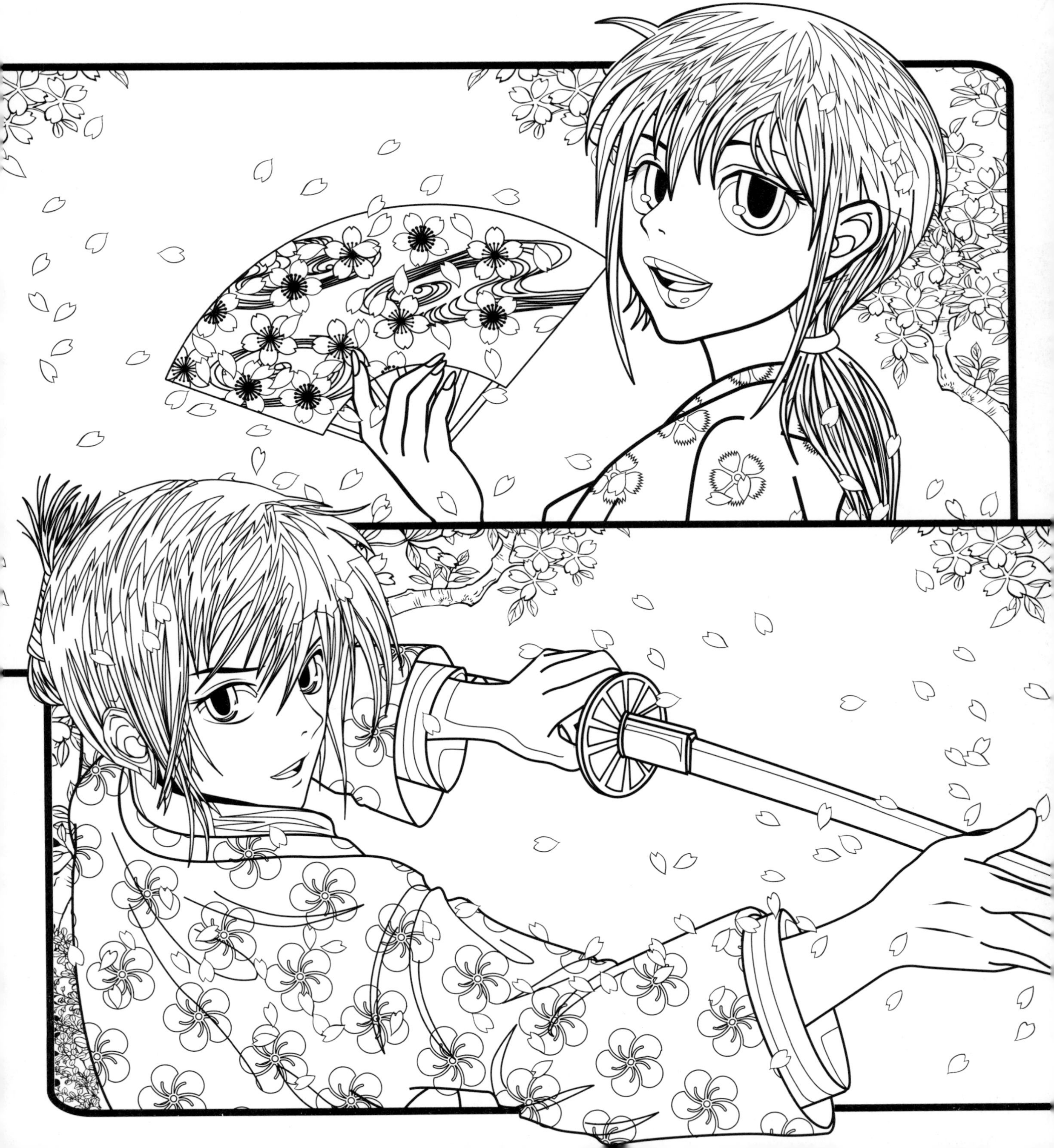

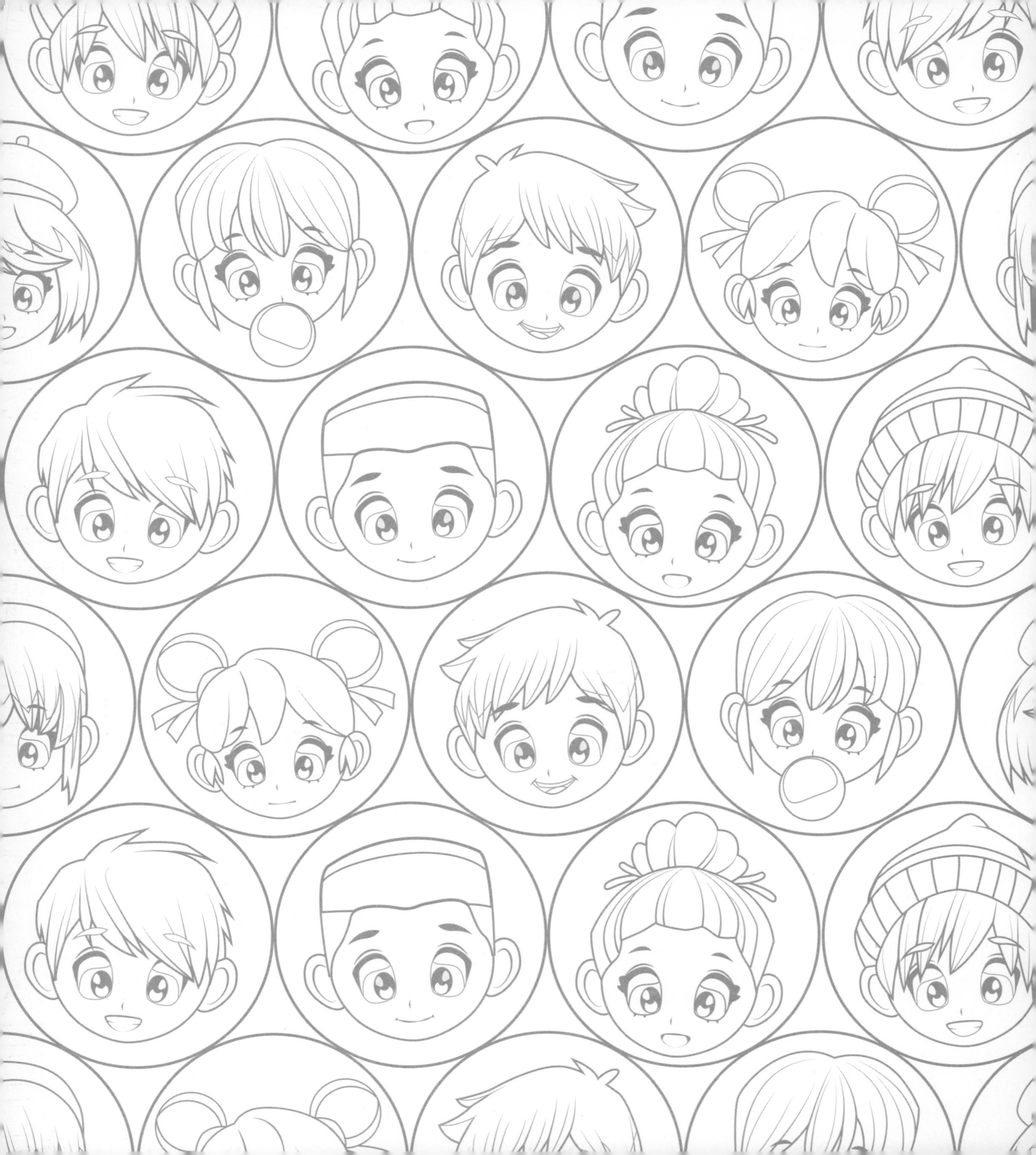

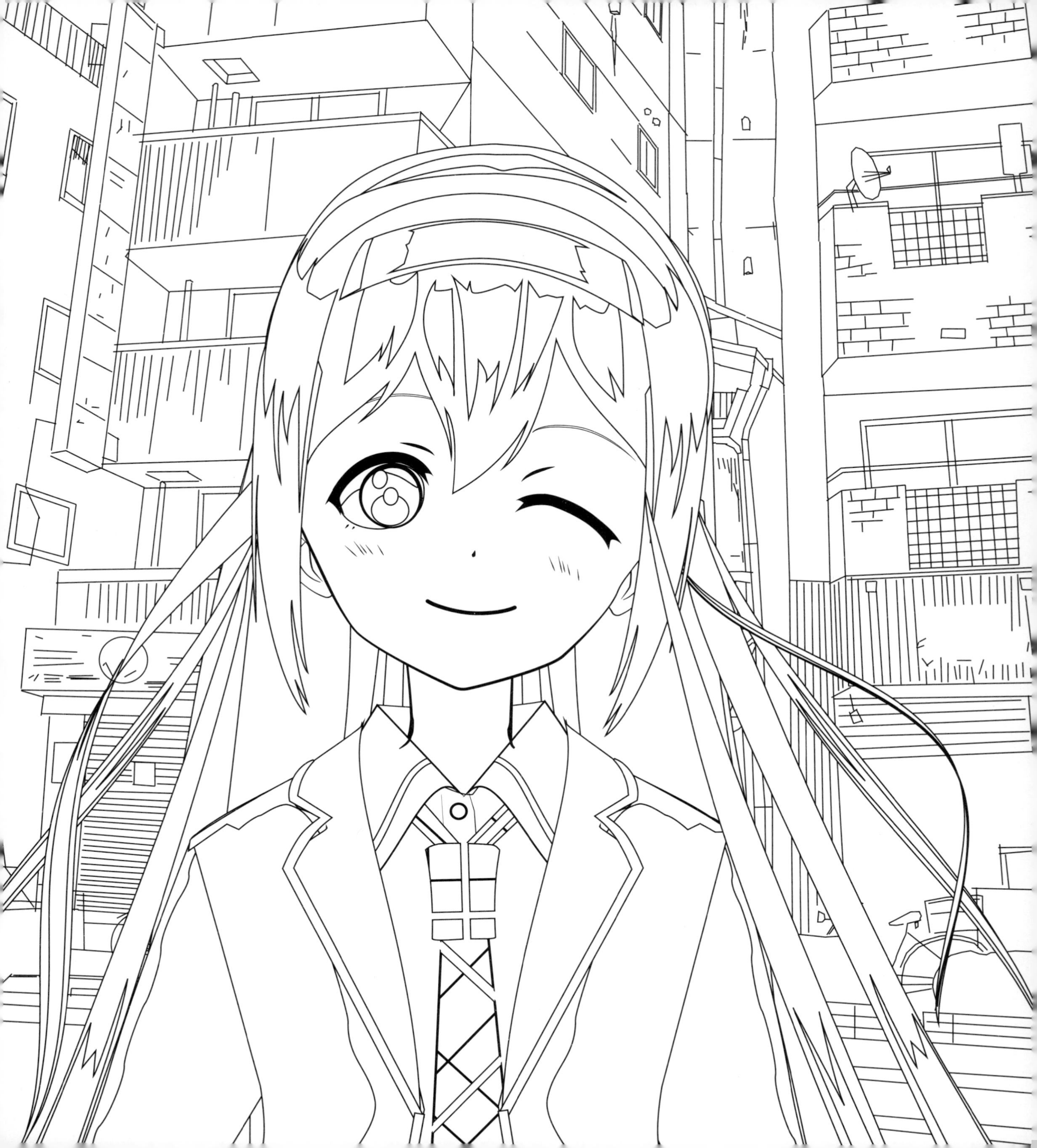

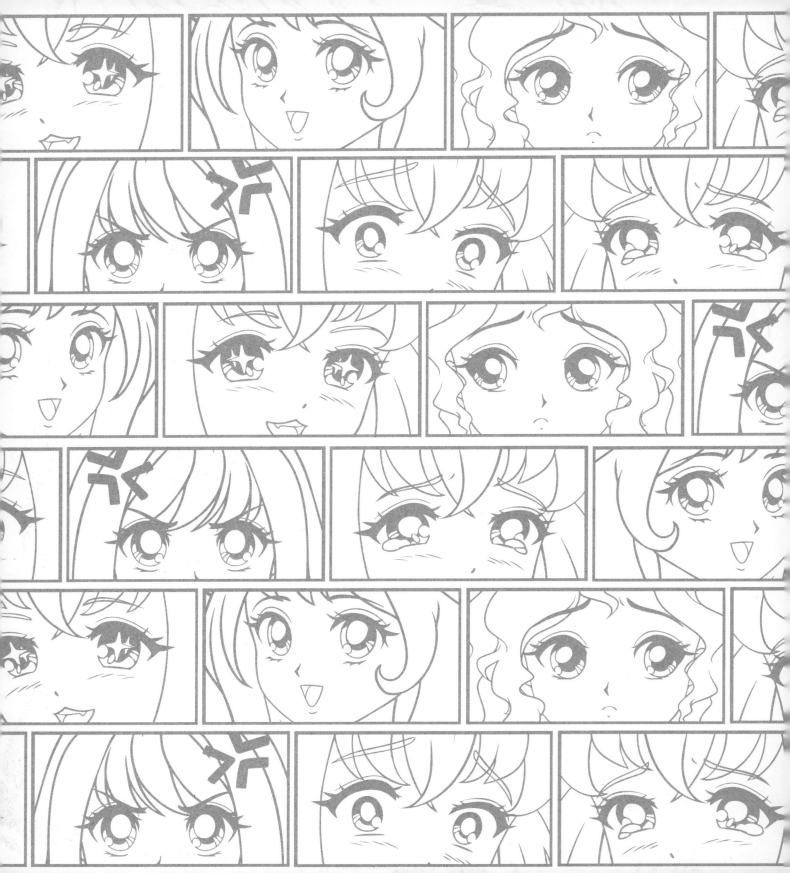

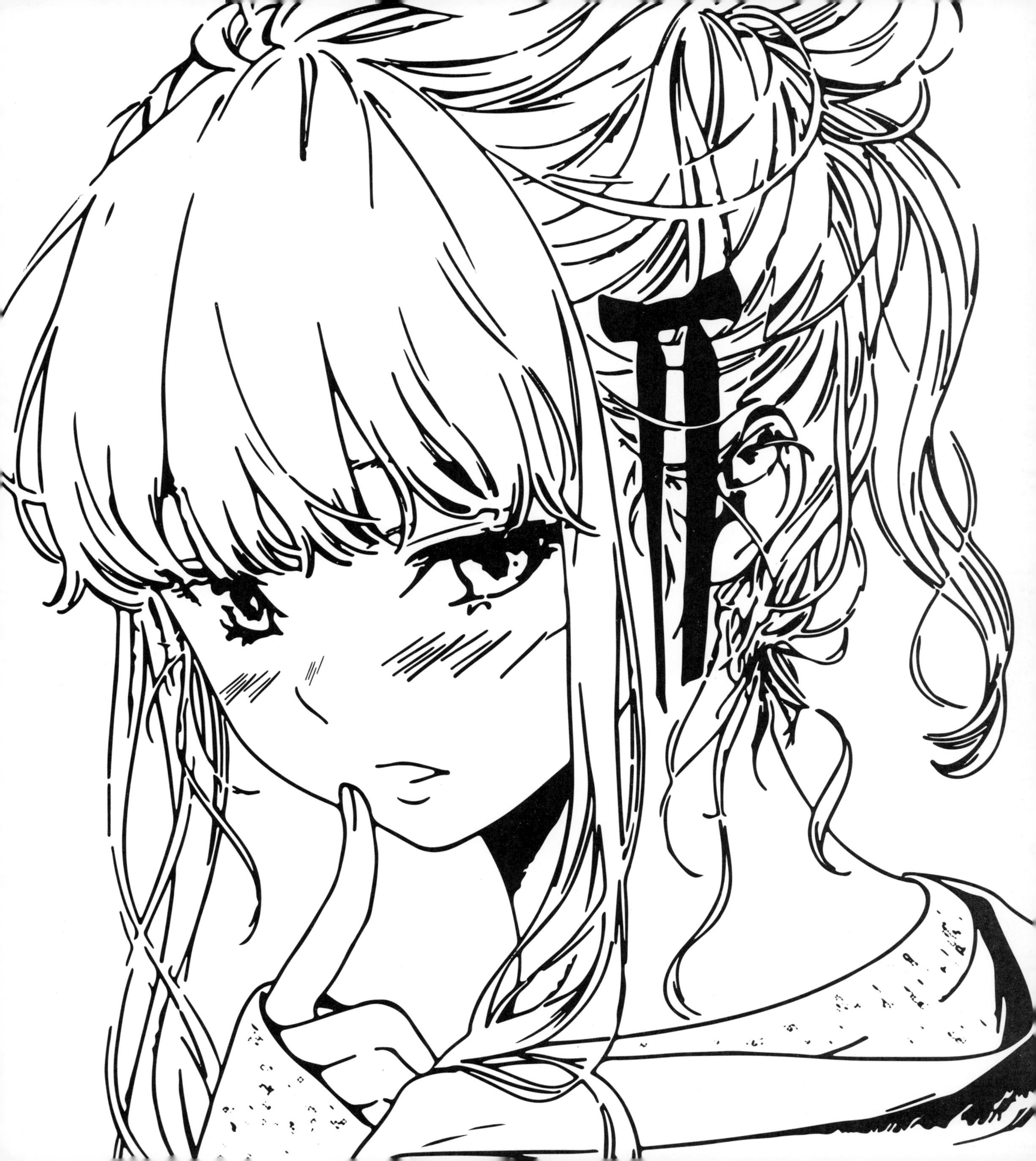

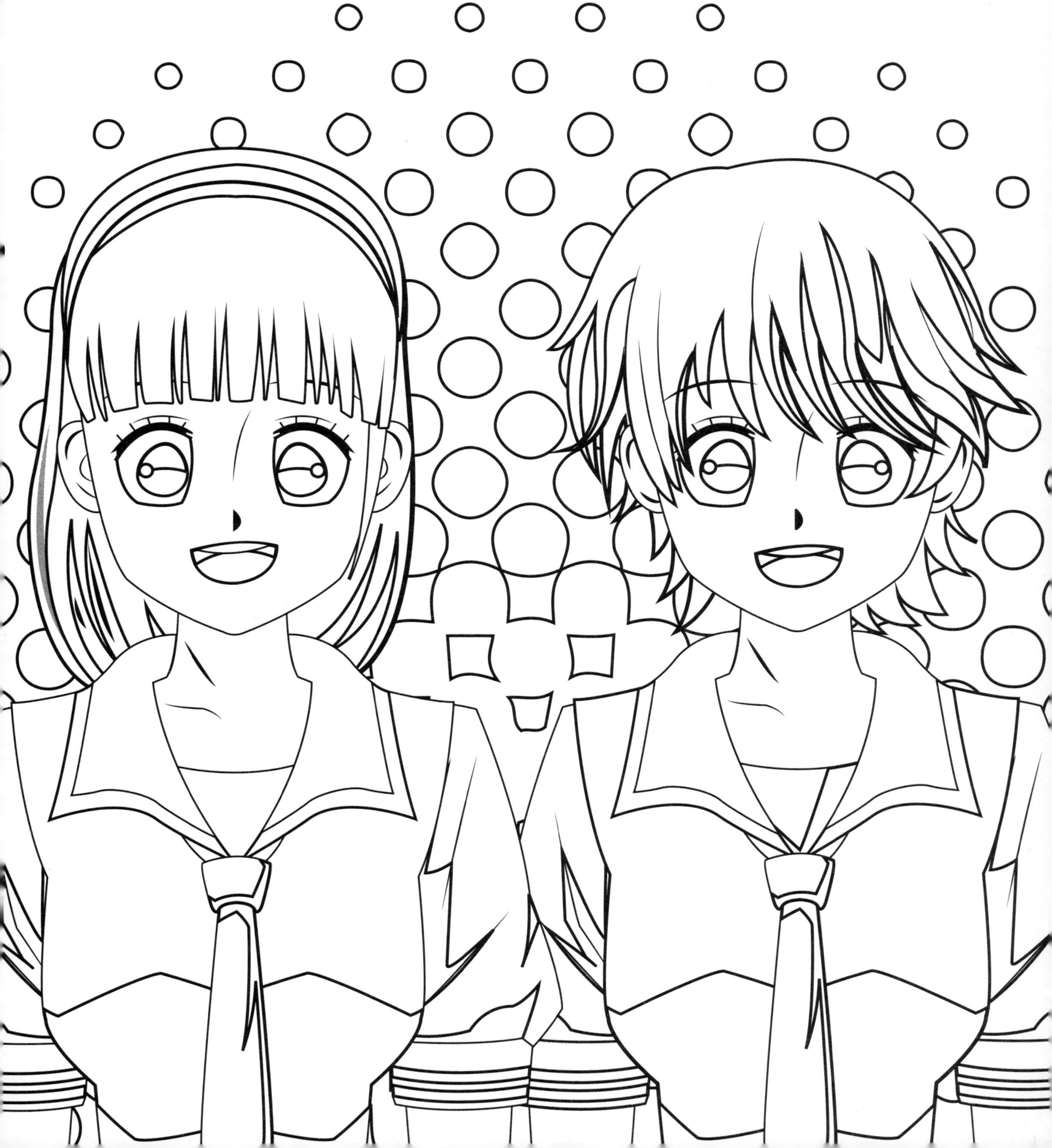

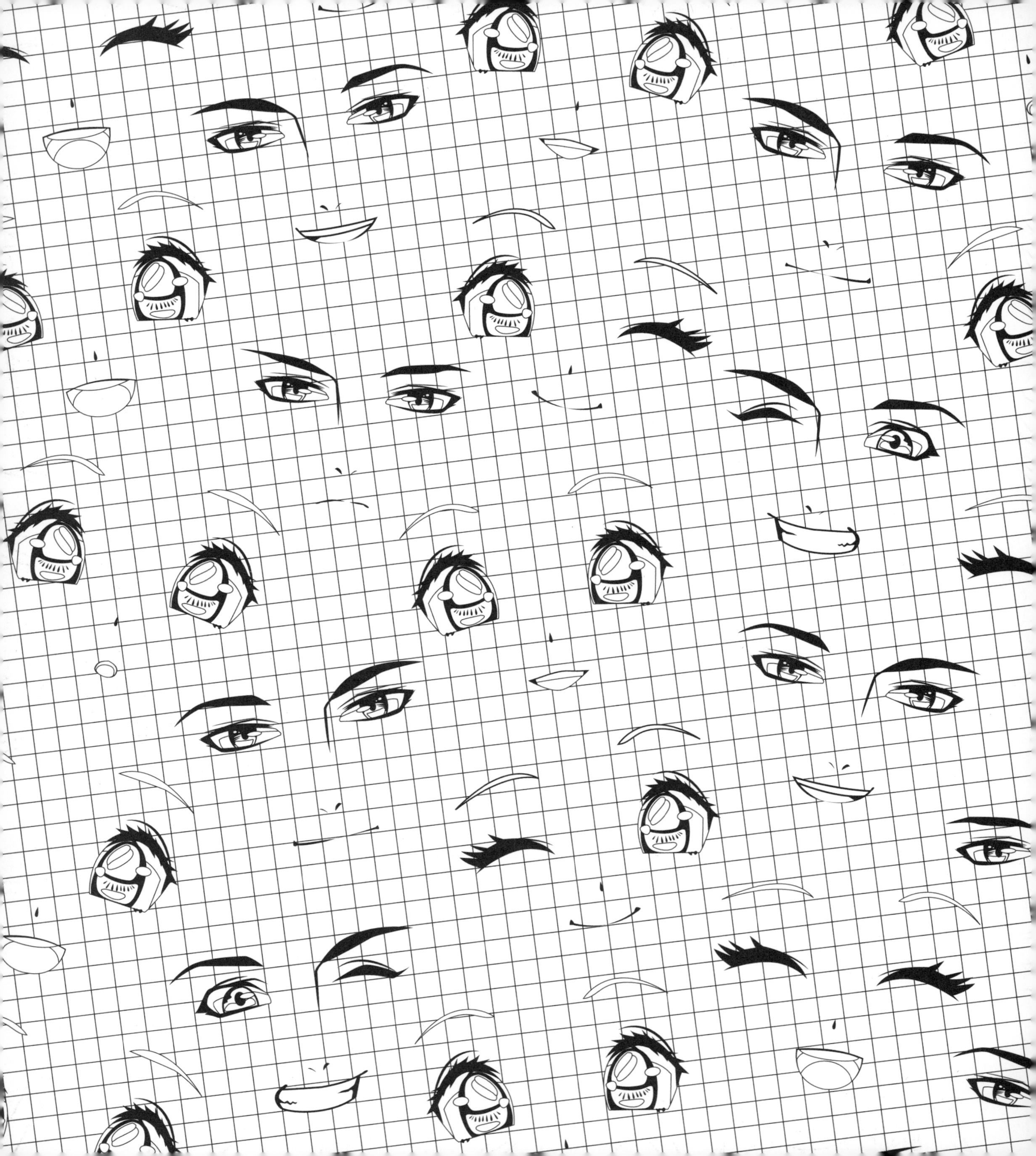

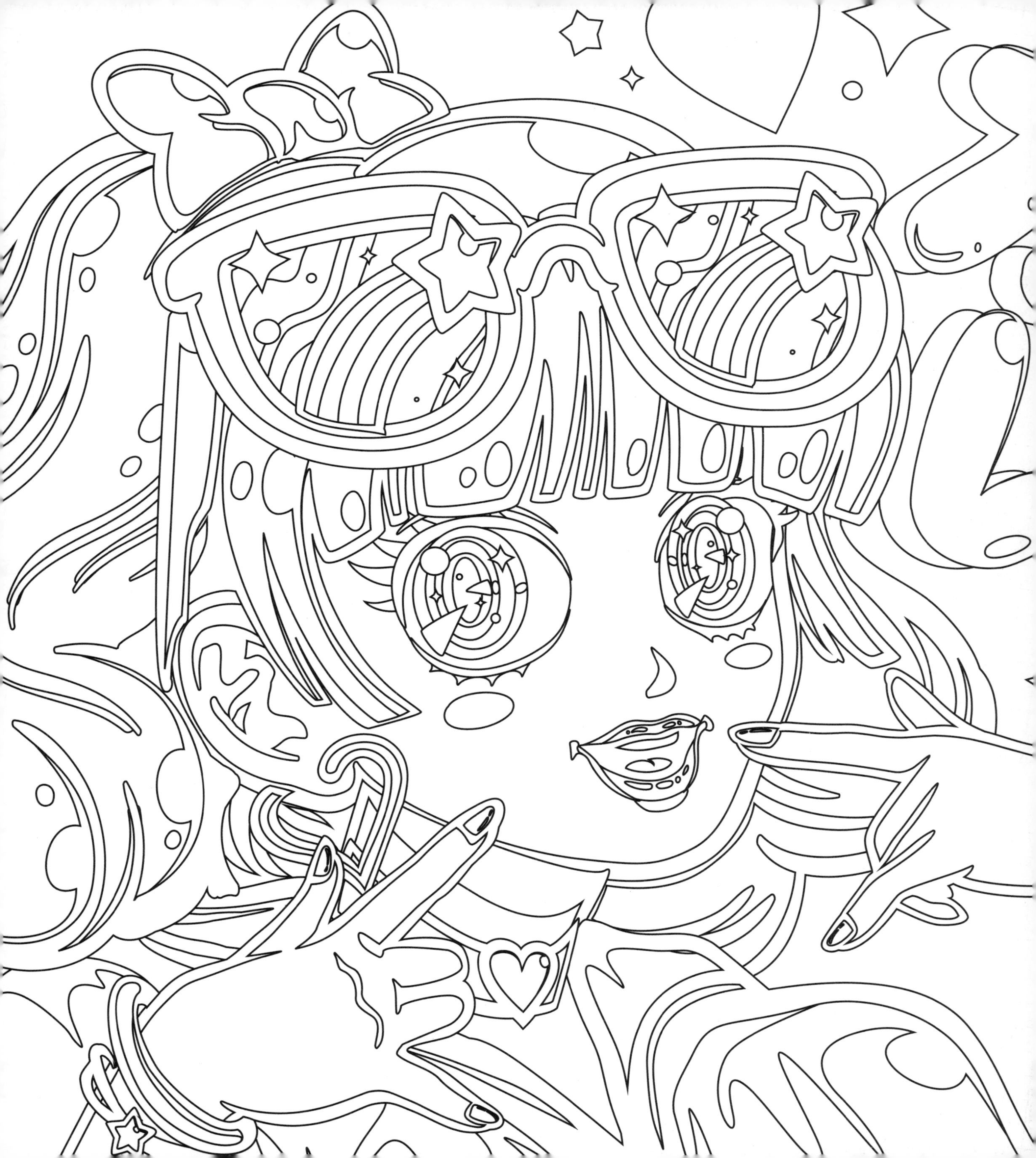

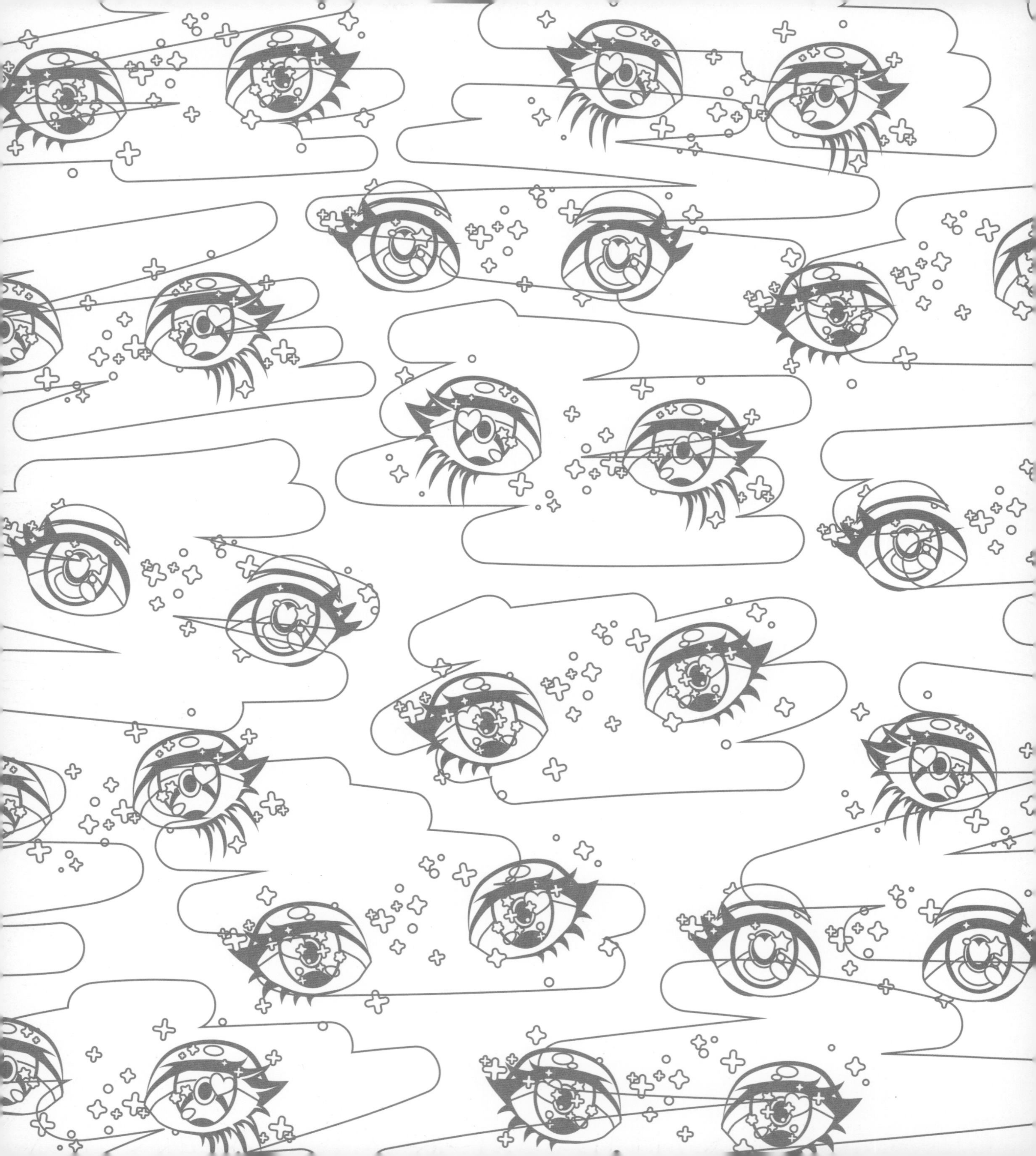

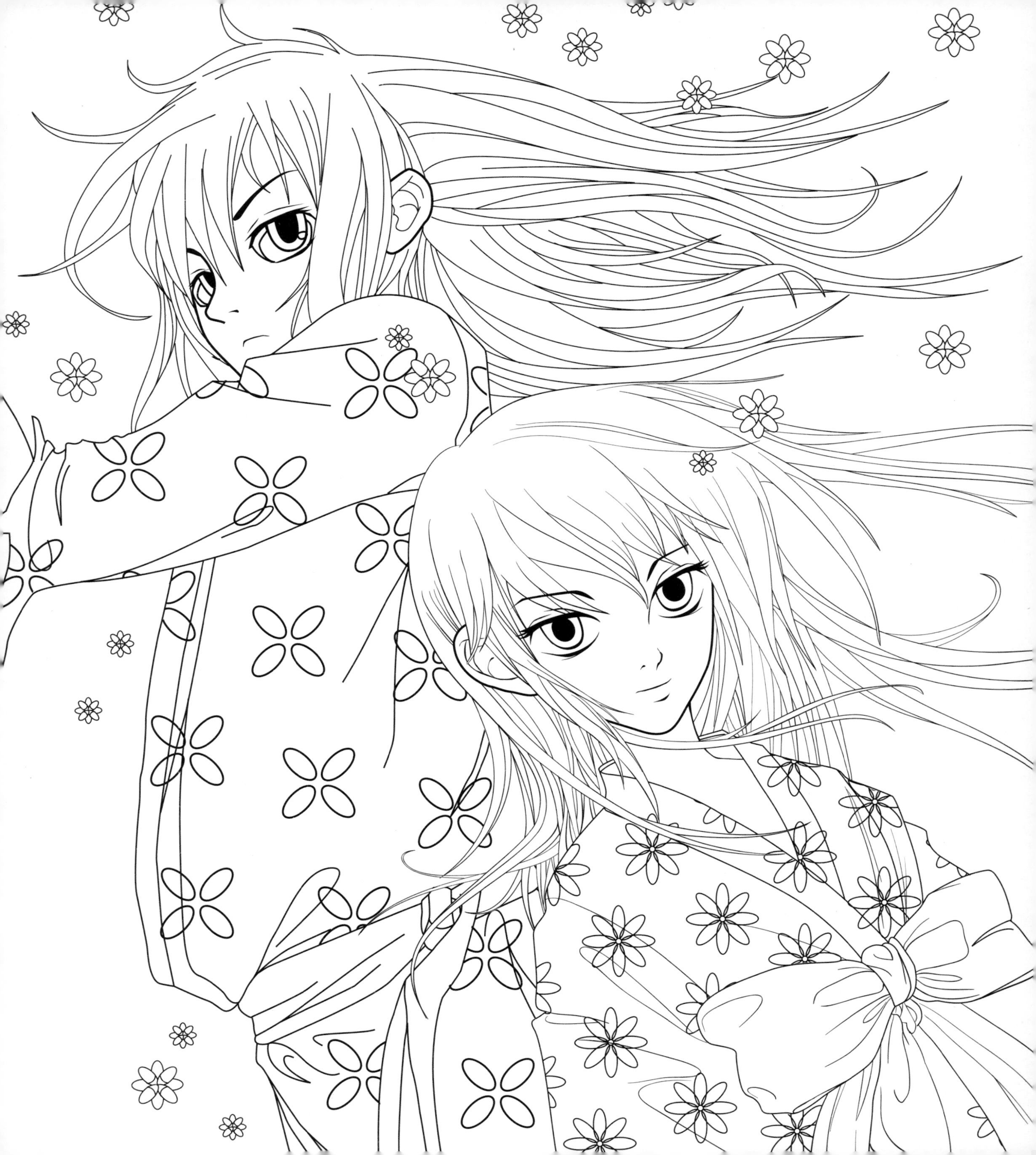

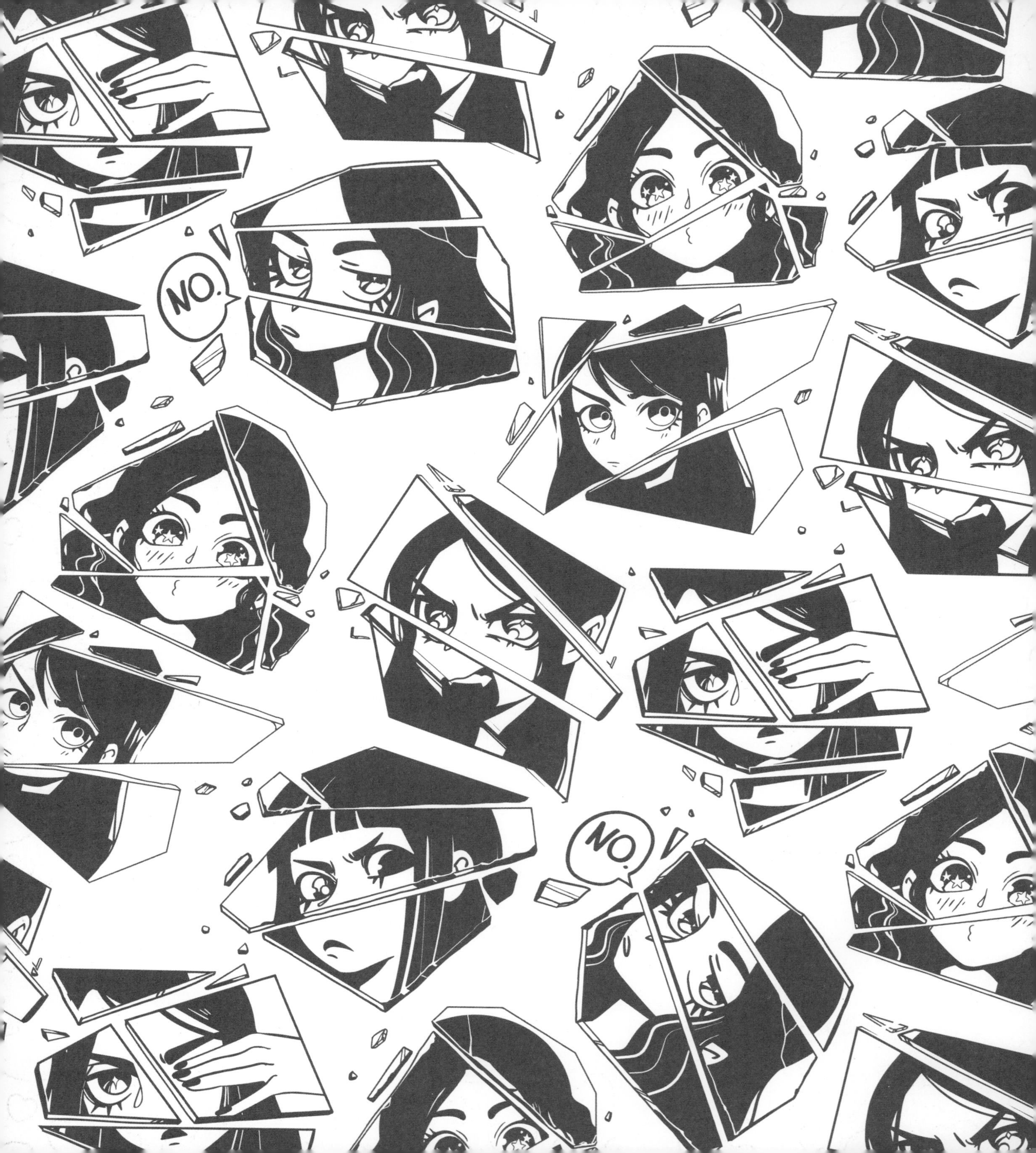
NO.
NO.

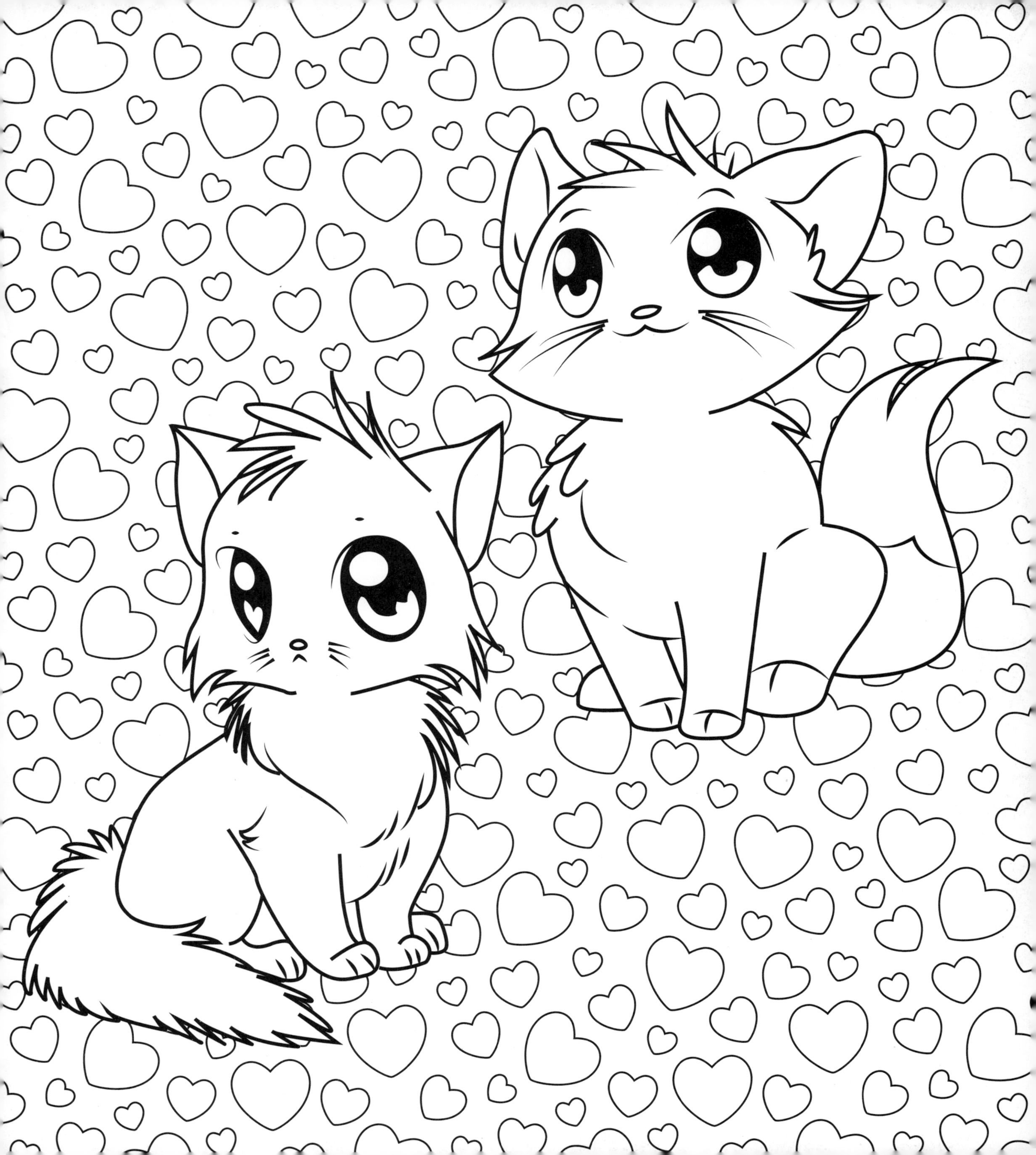

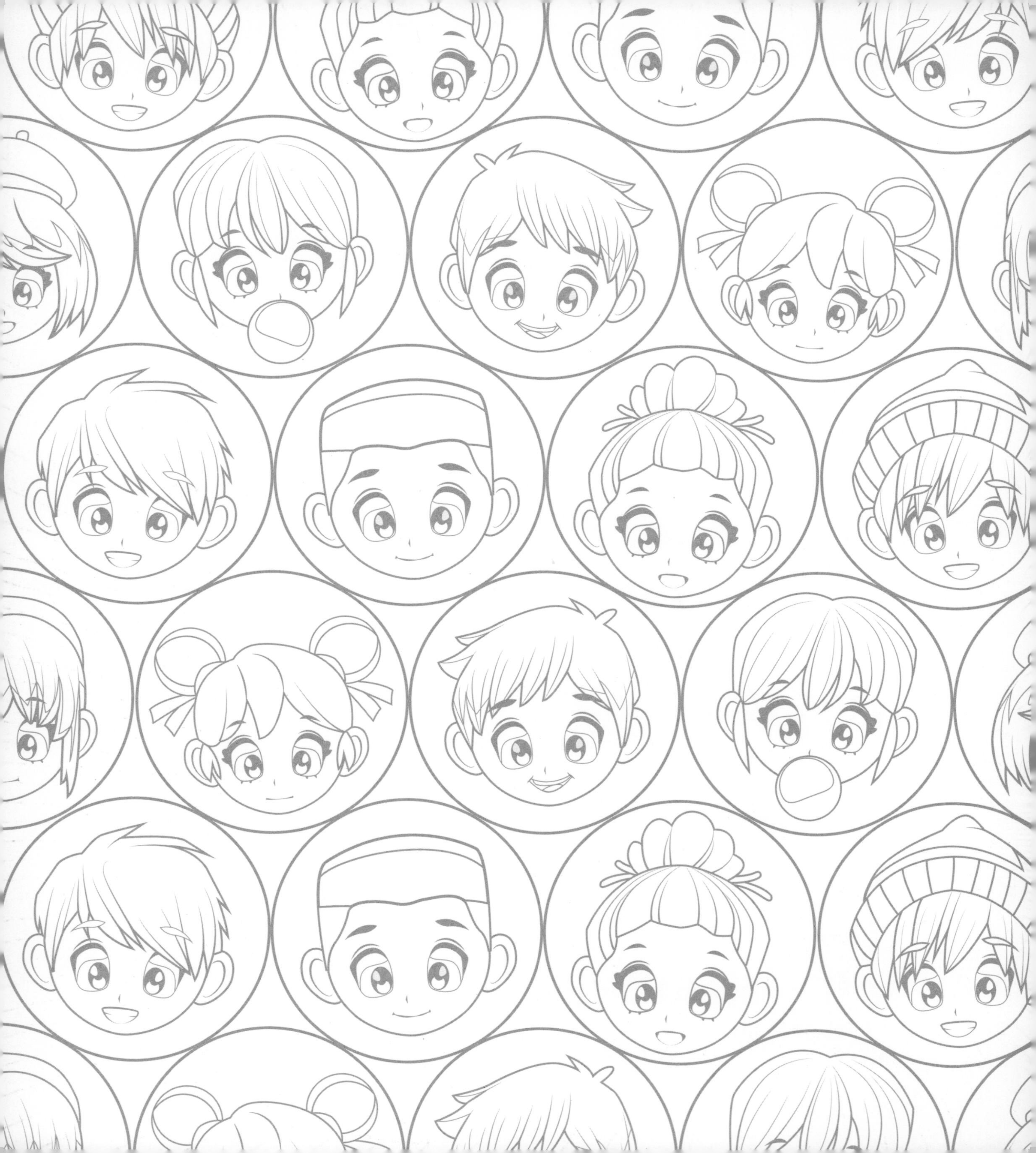

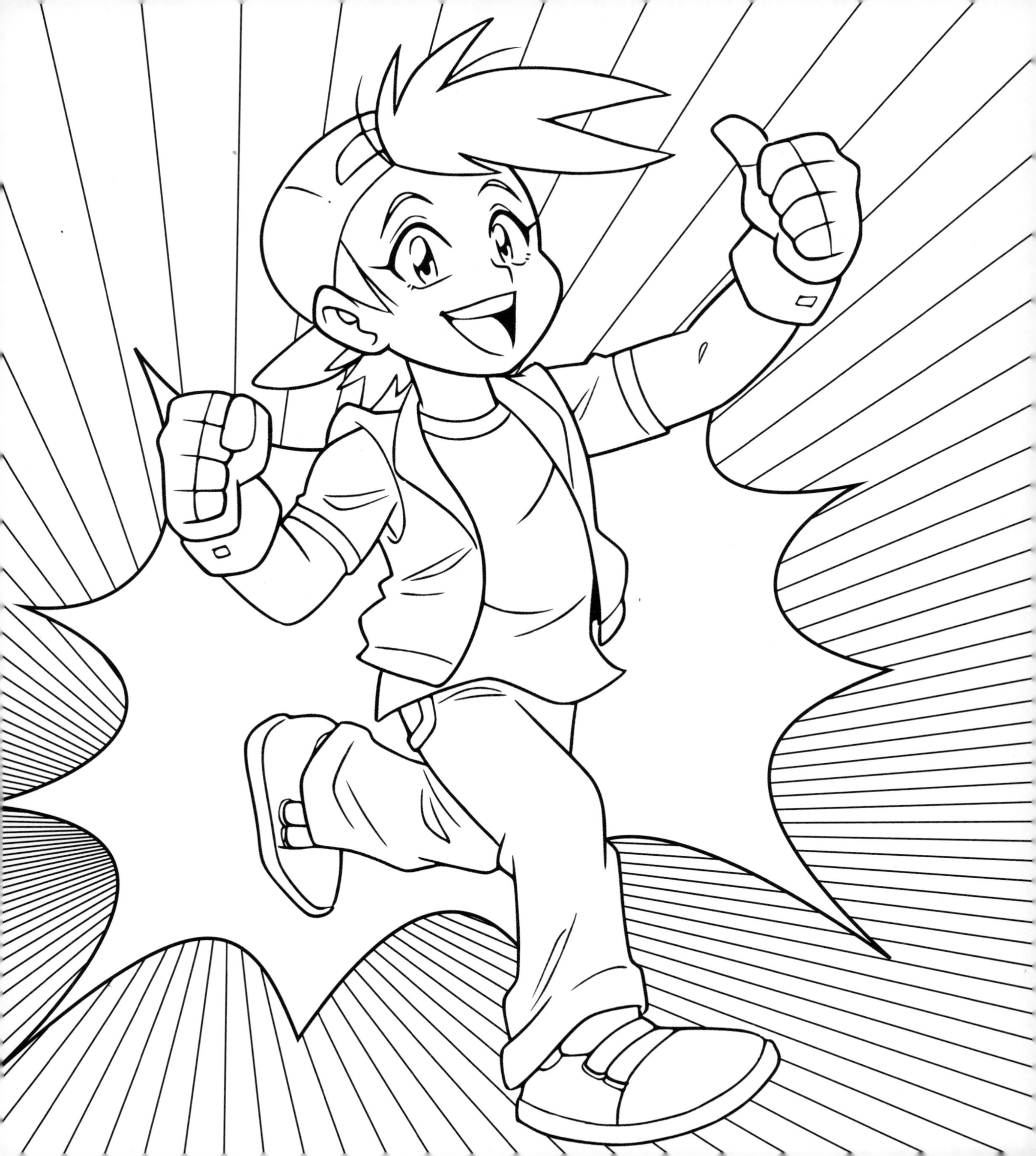

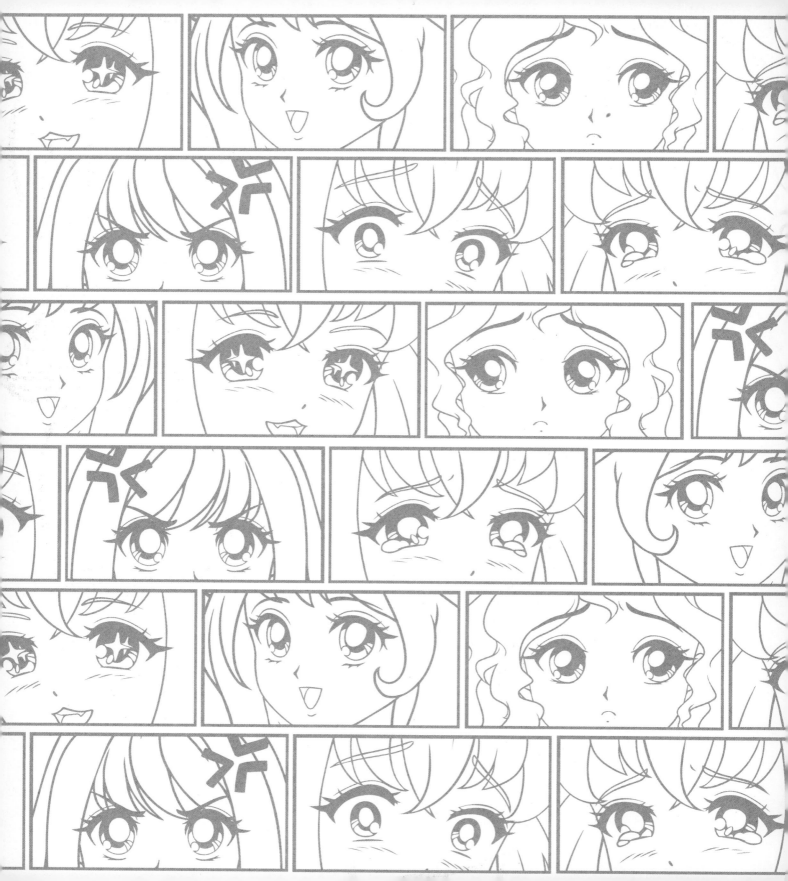

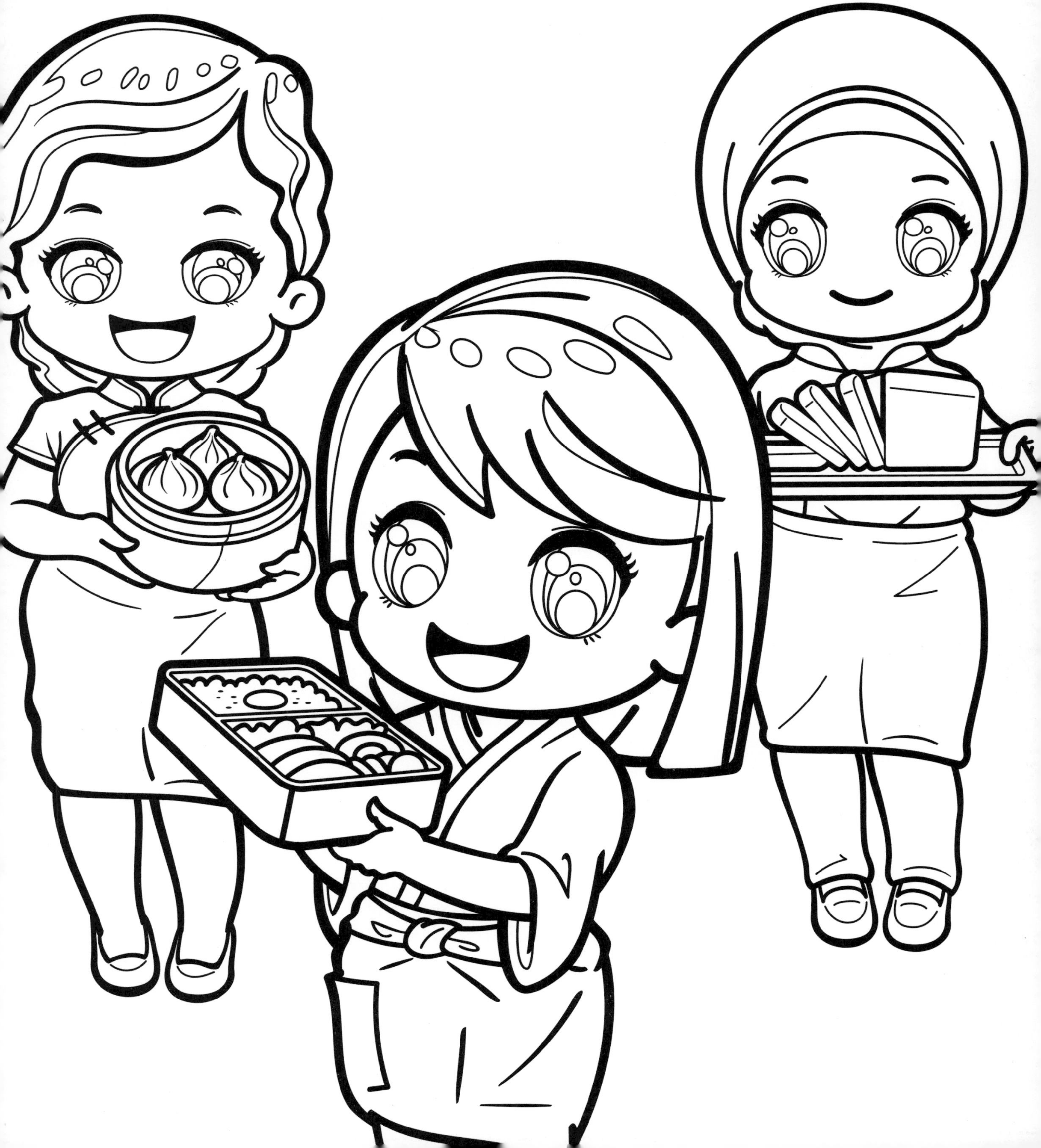

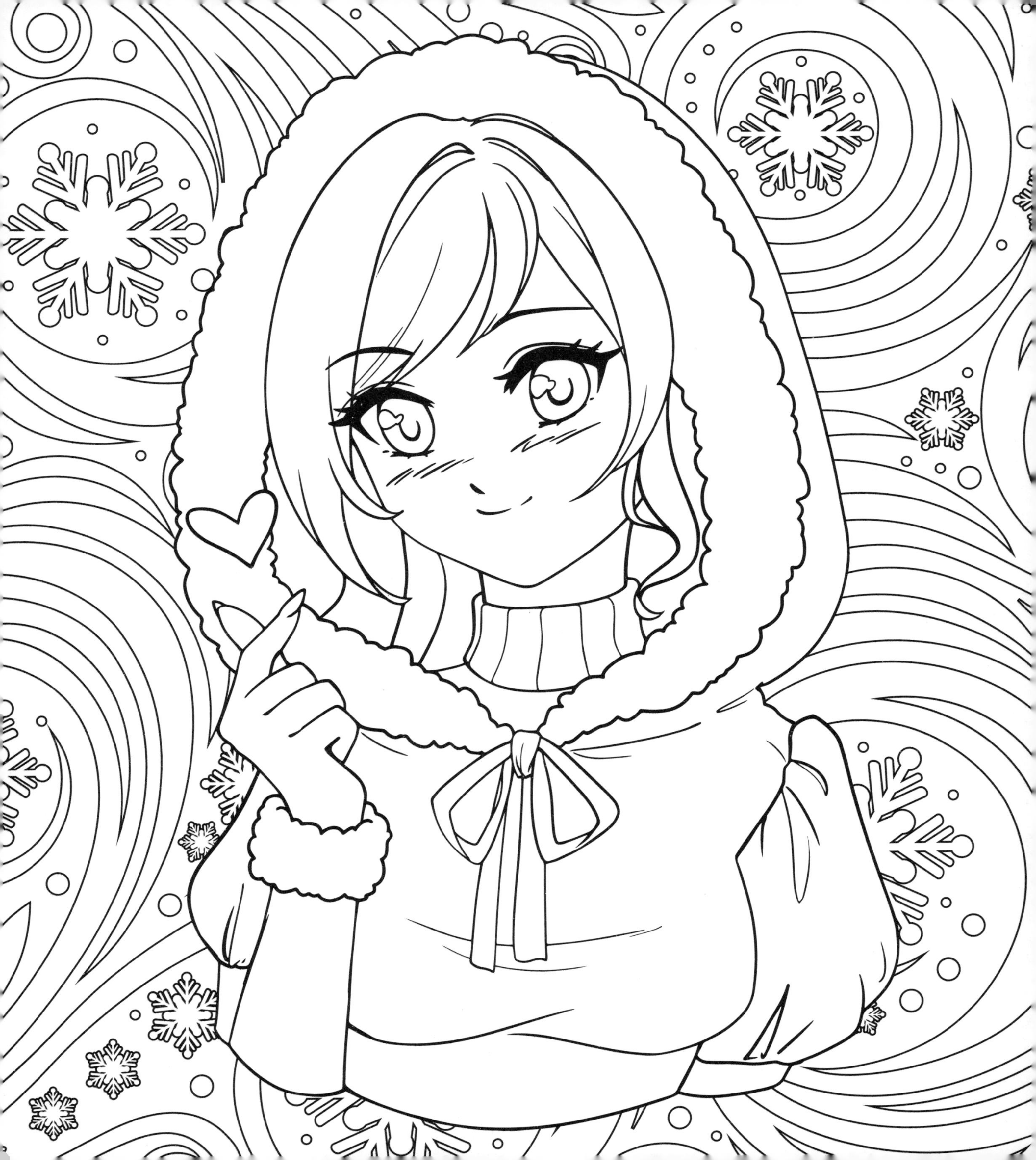

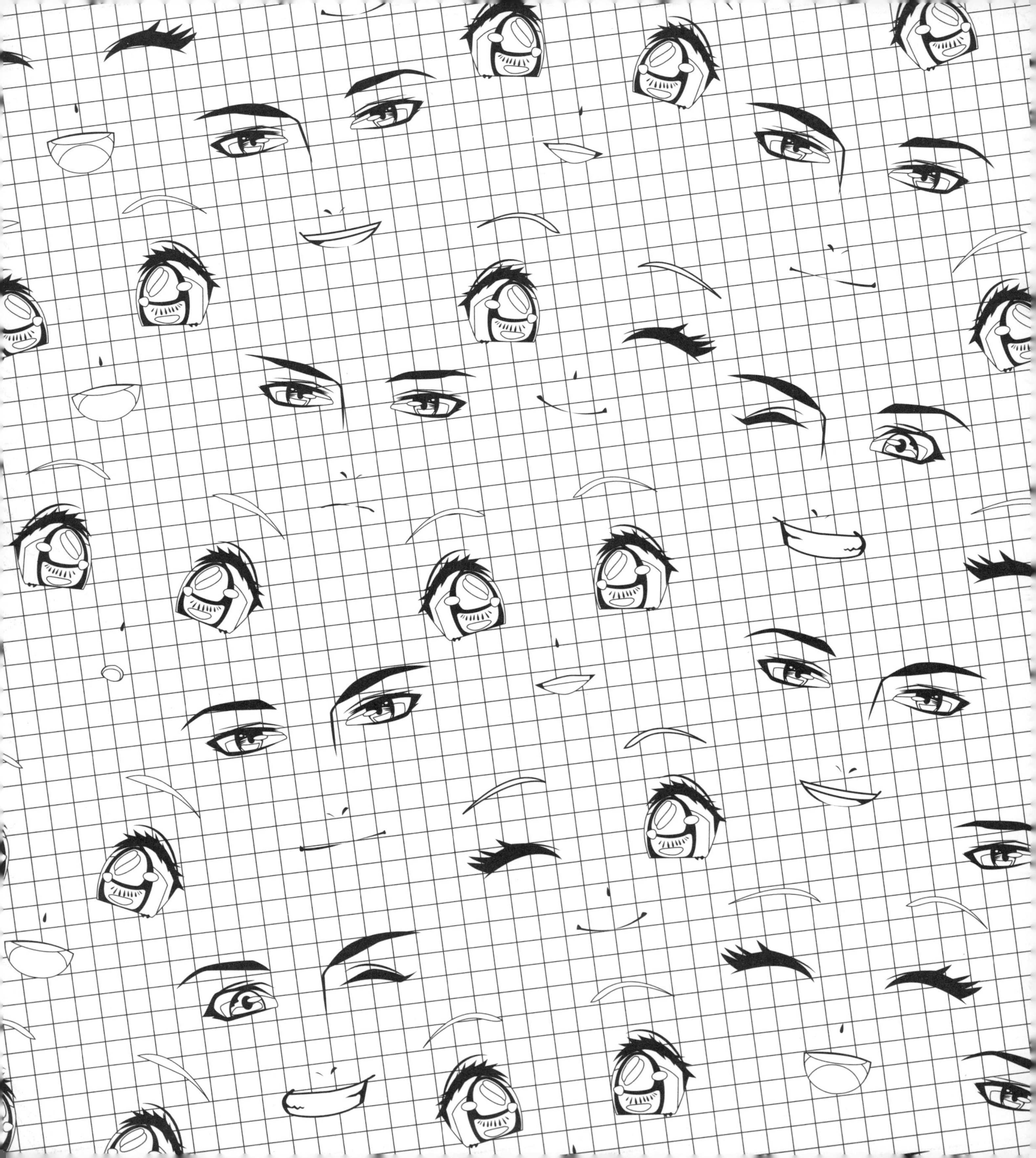

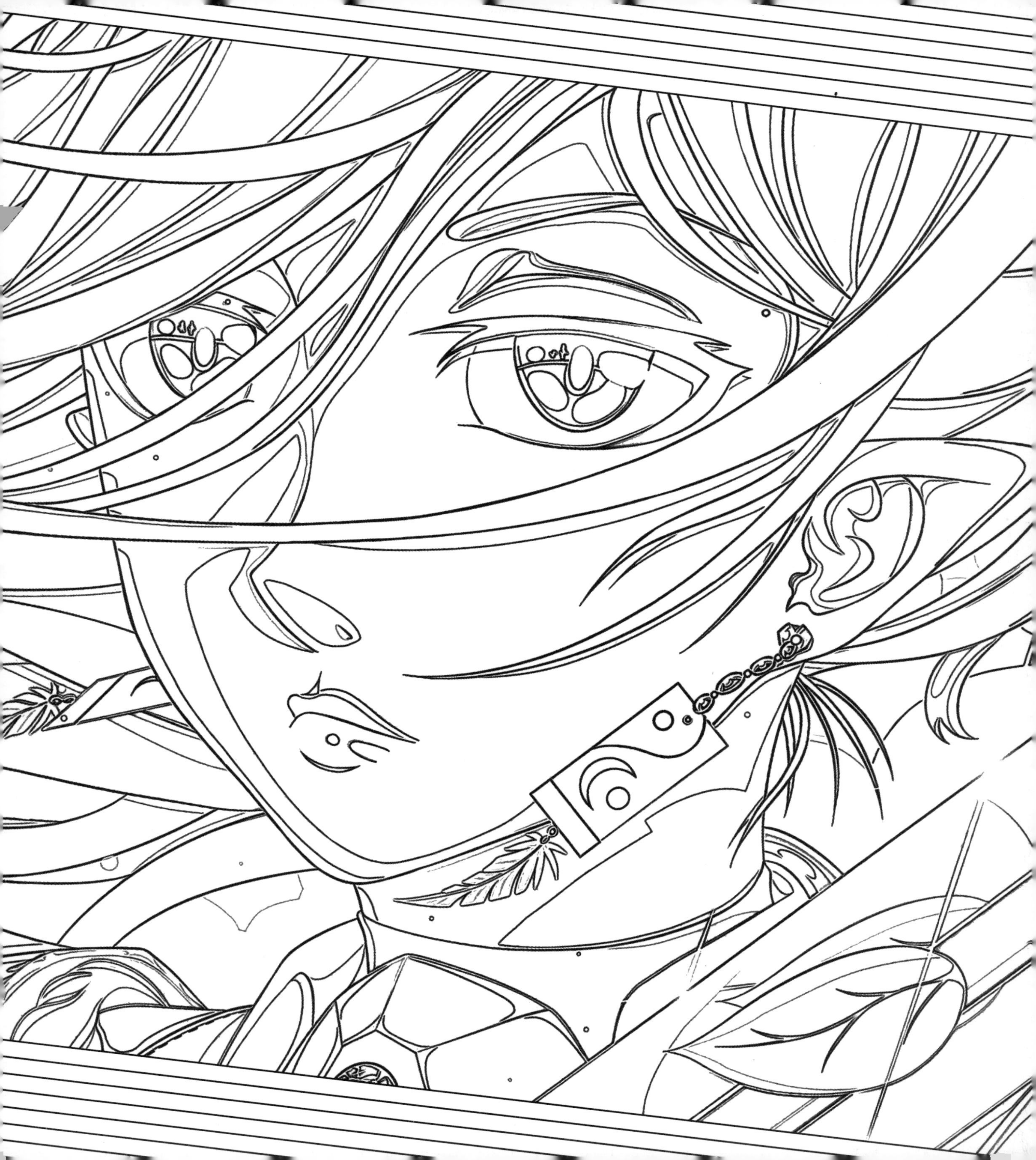

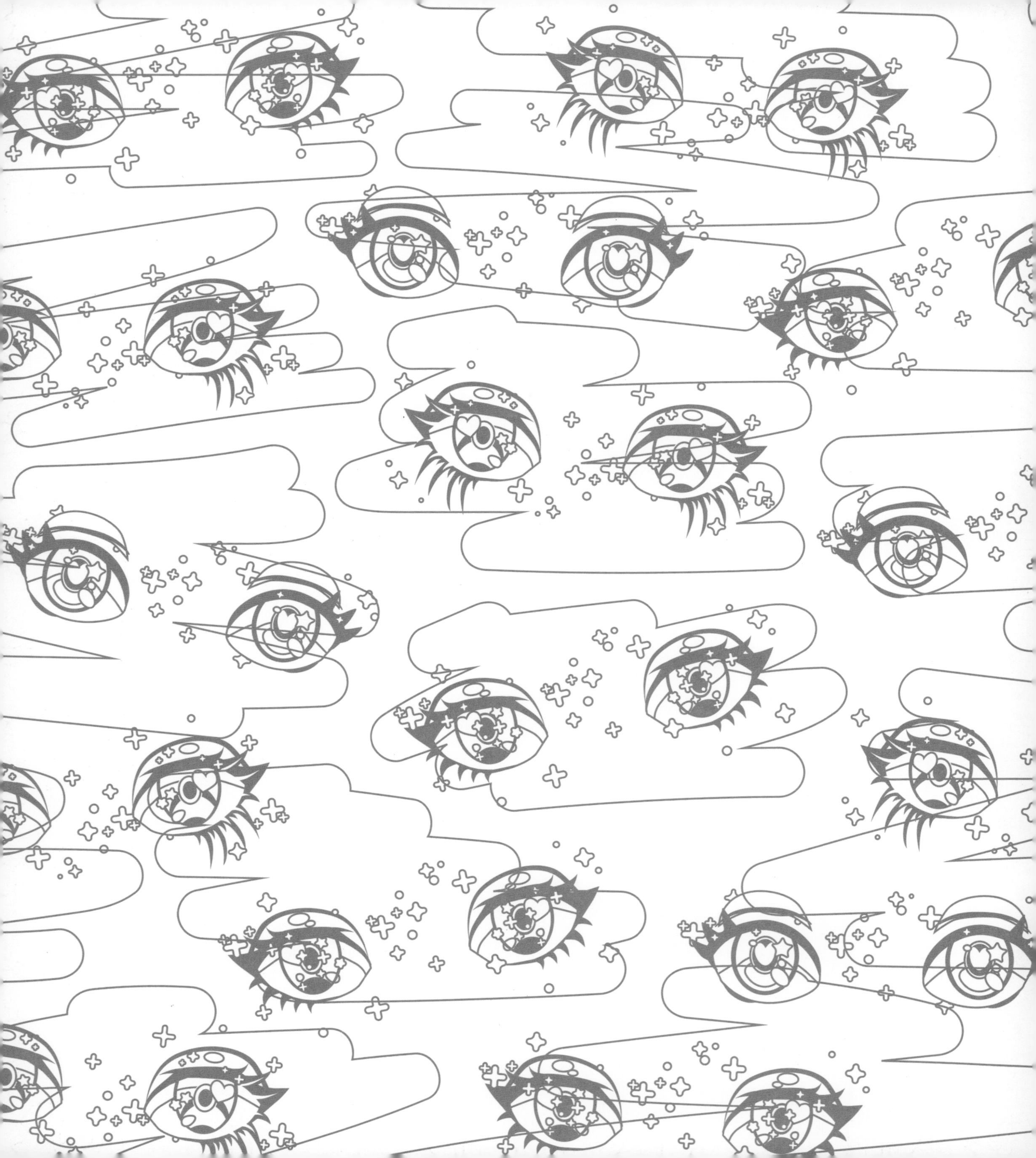

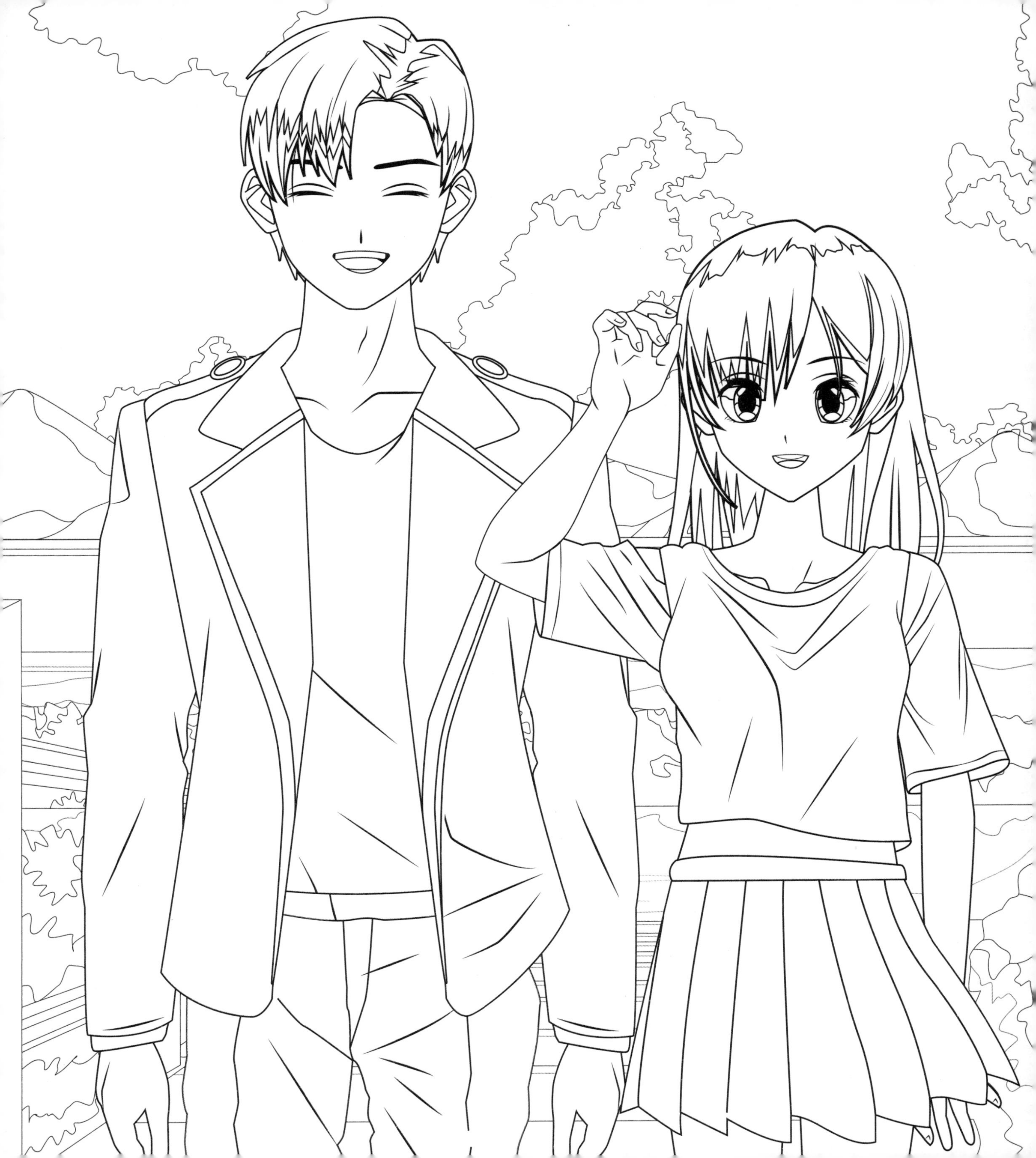

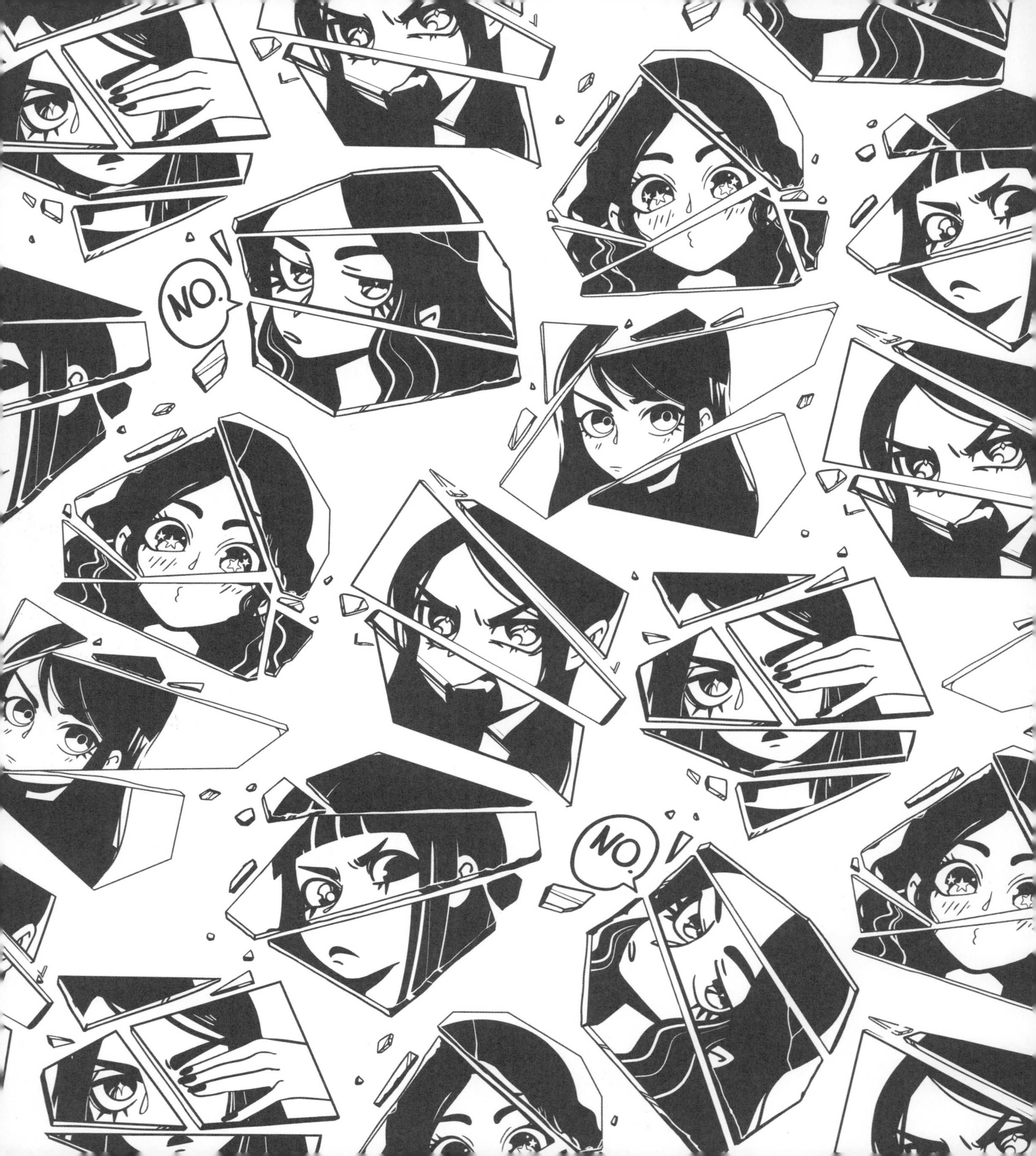
NO.
NO.

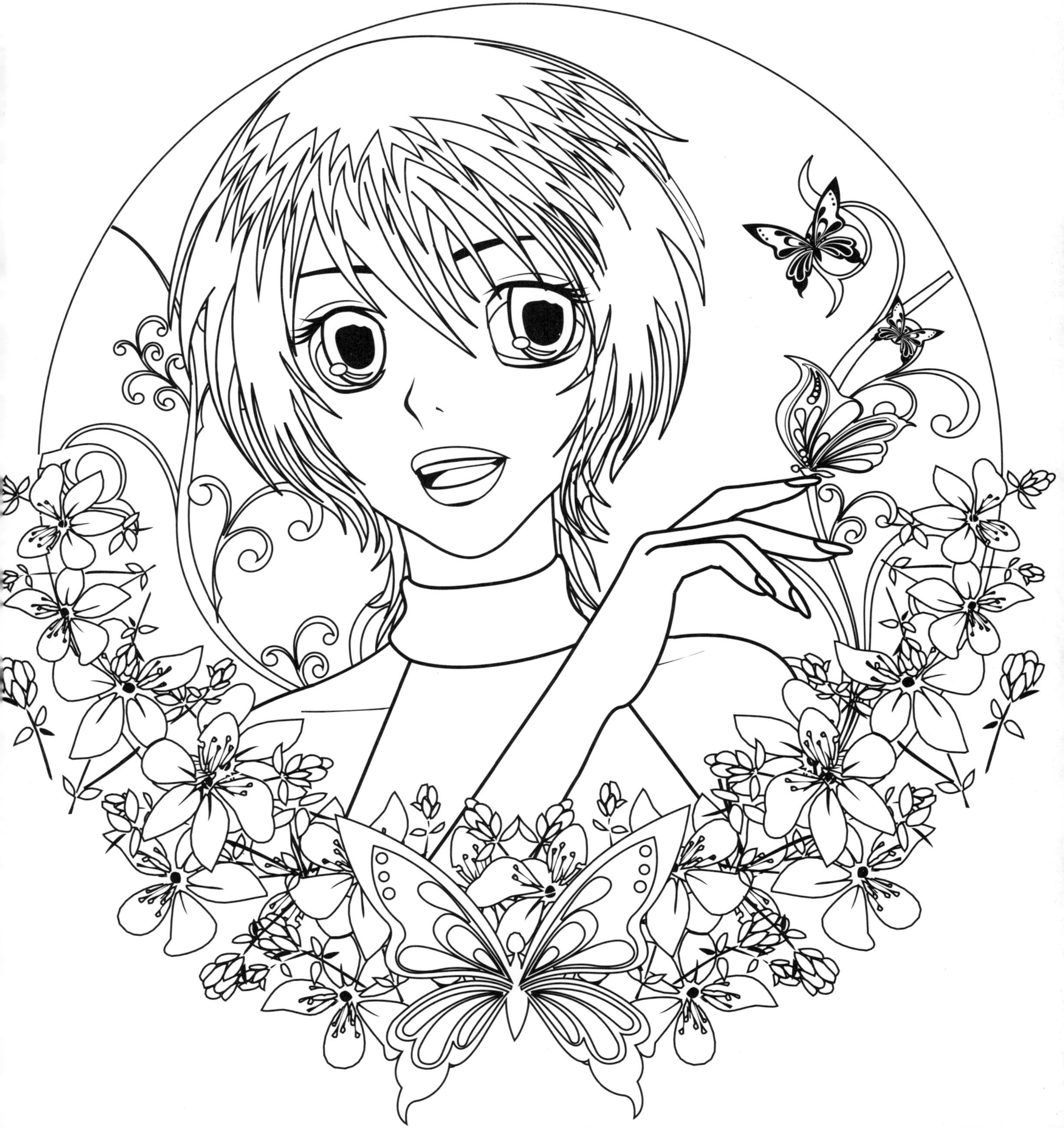

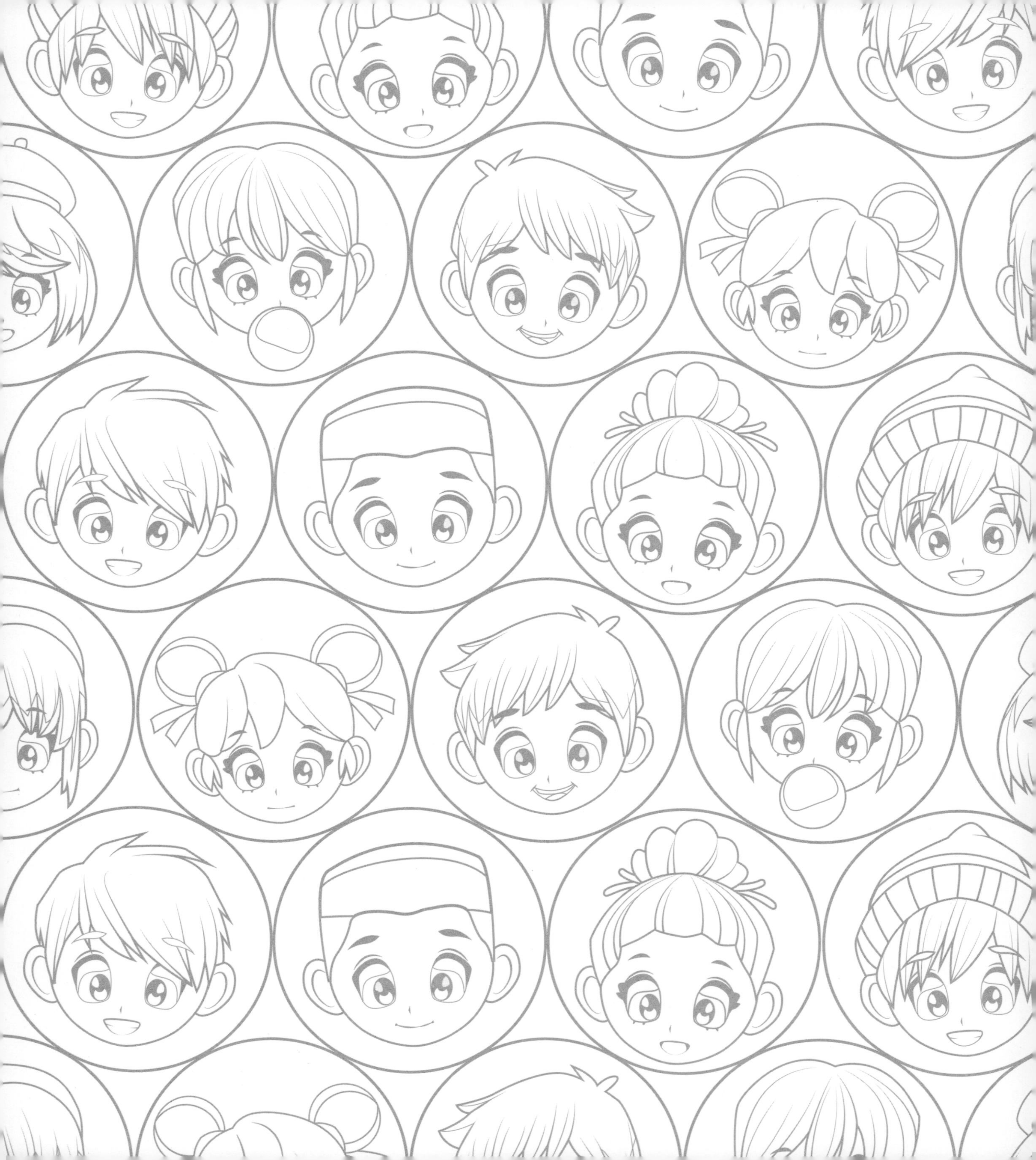

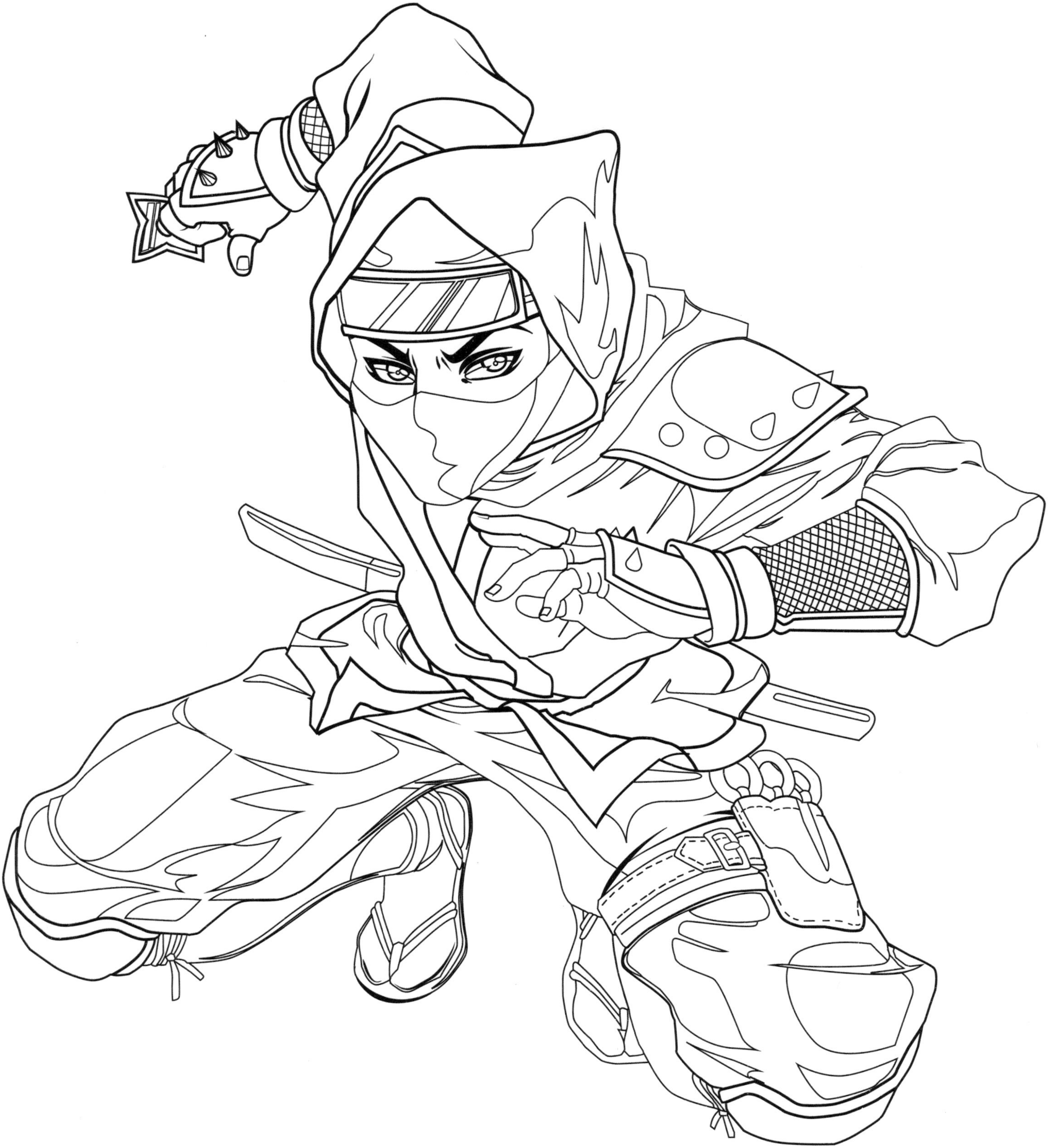

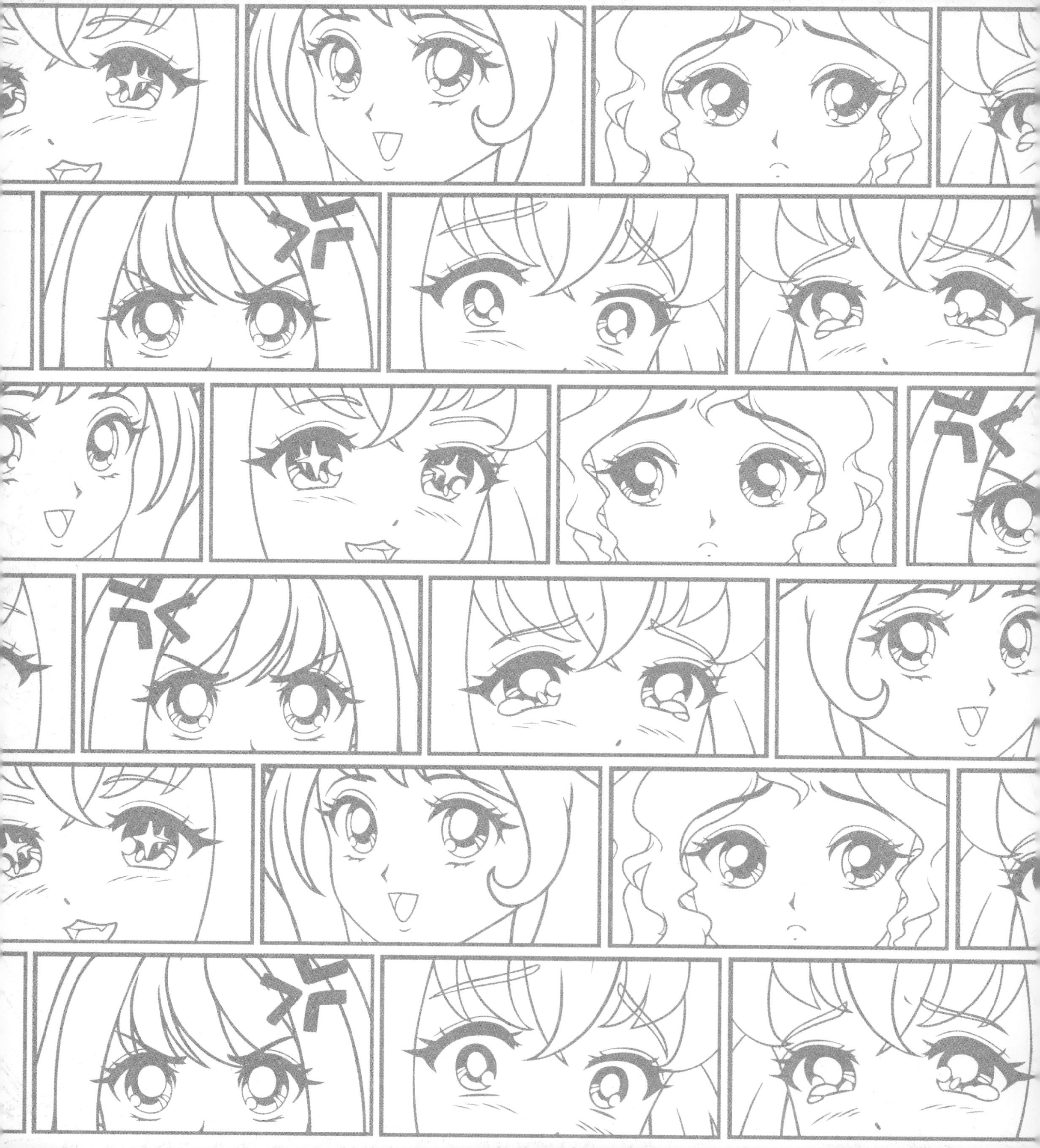

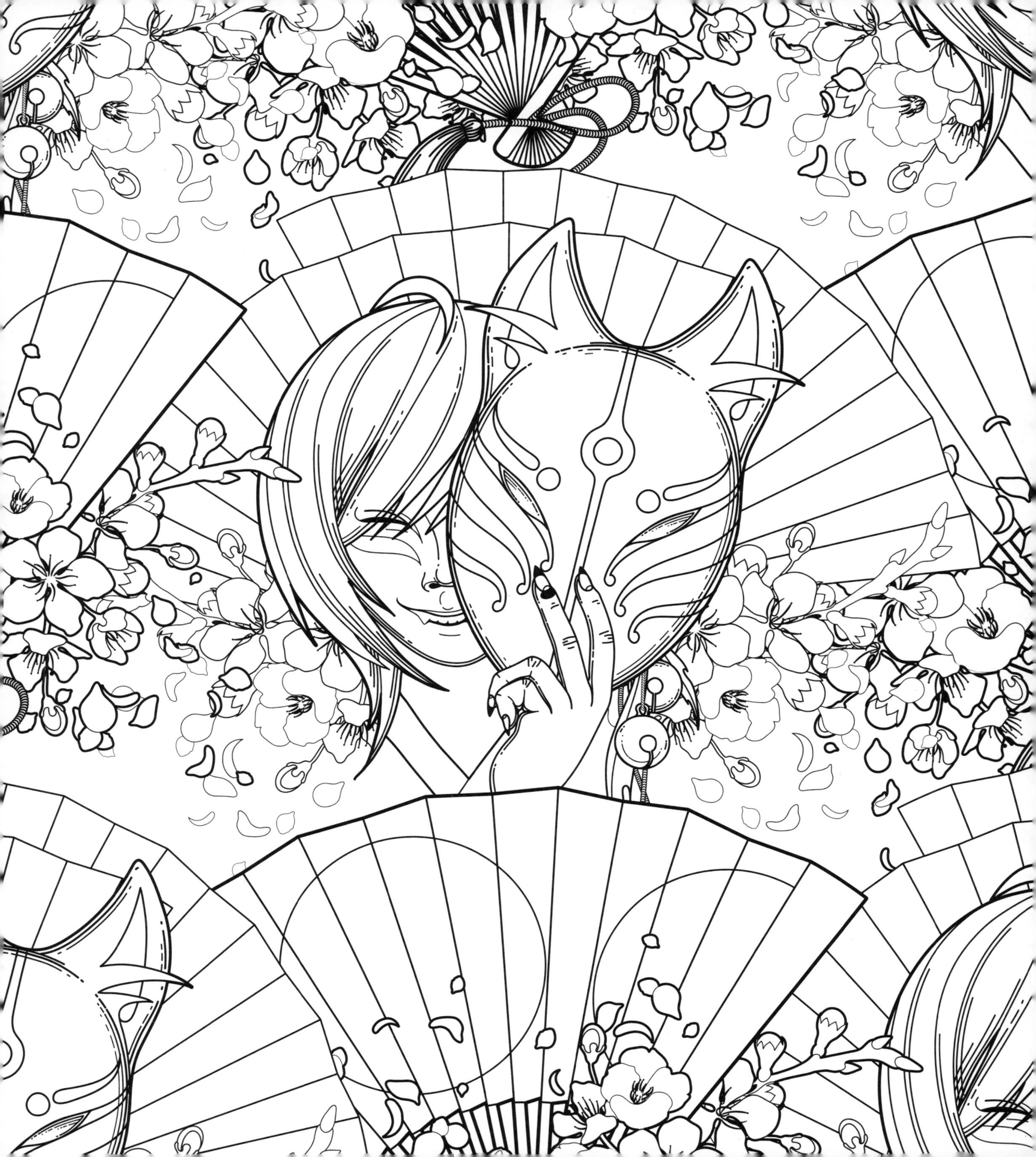

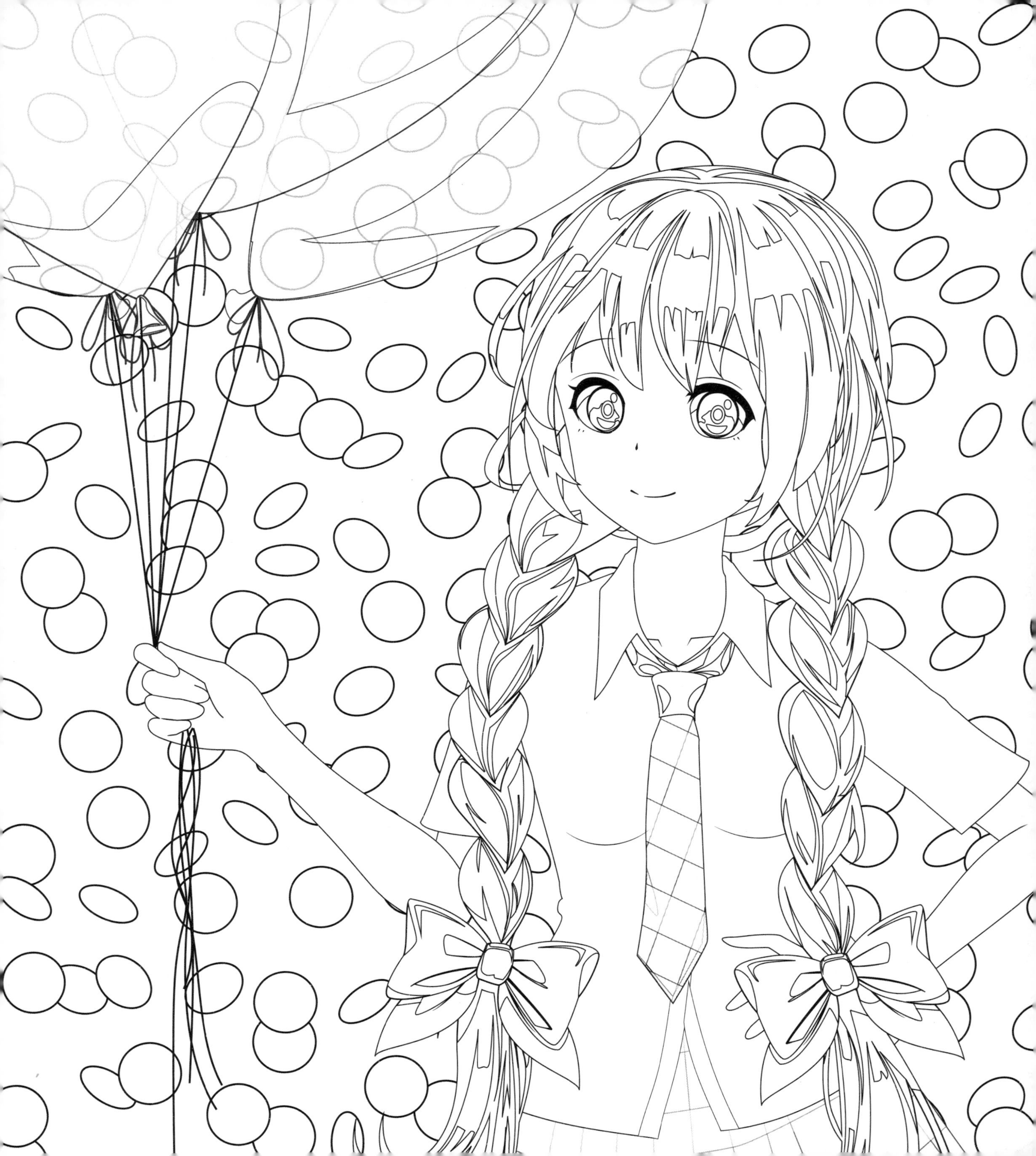

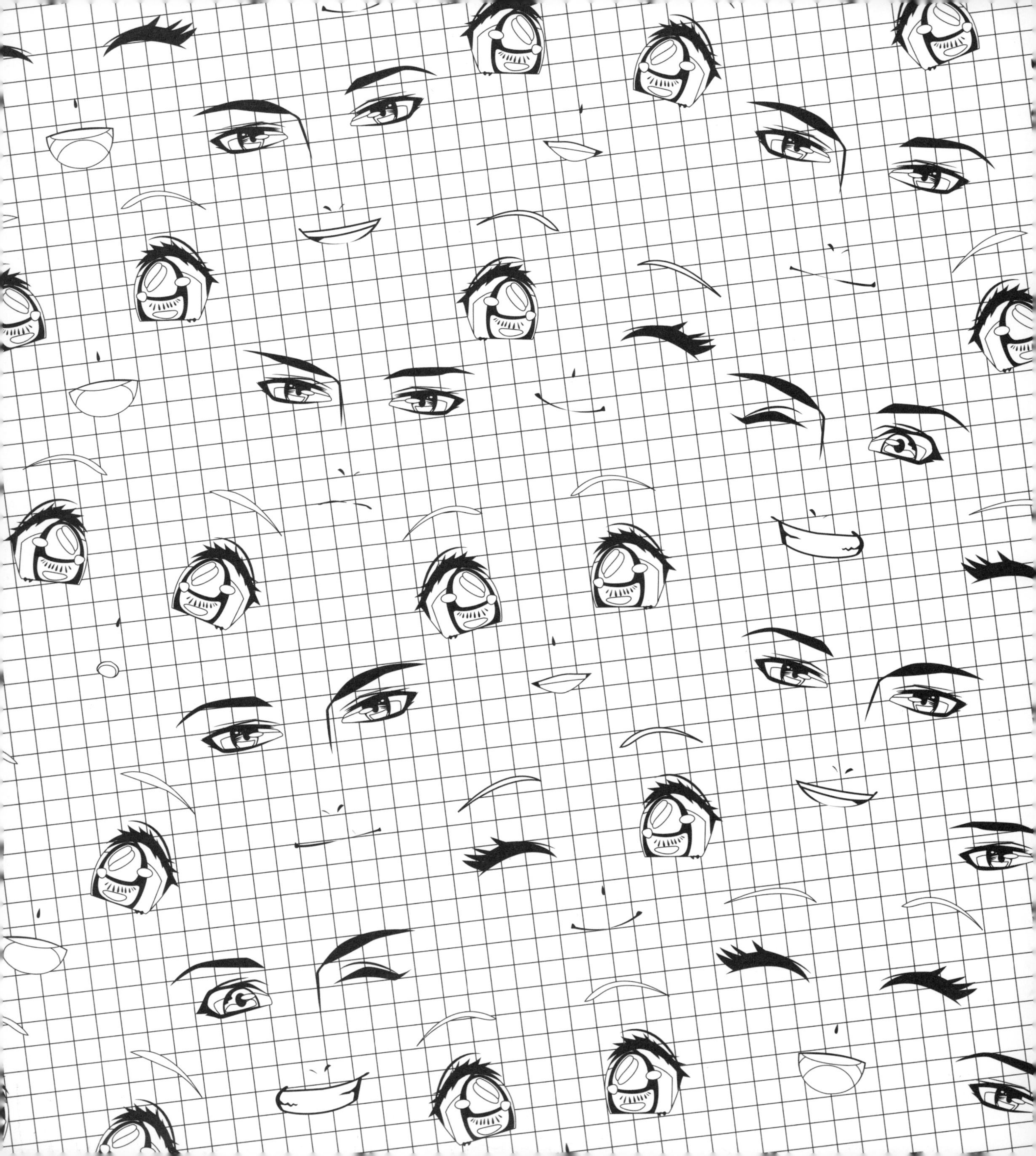

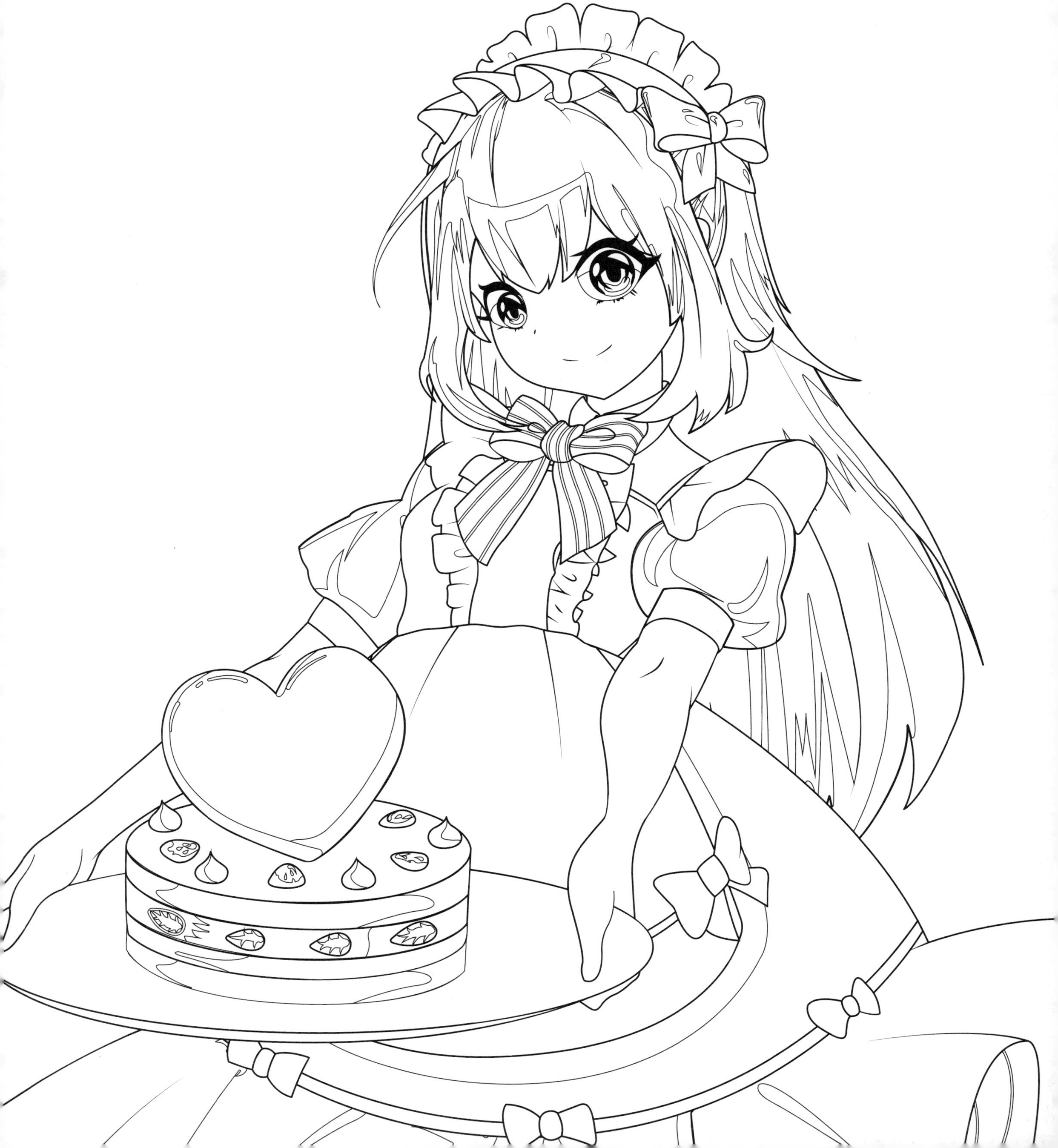

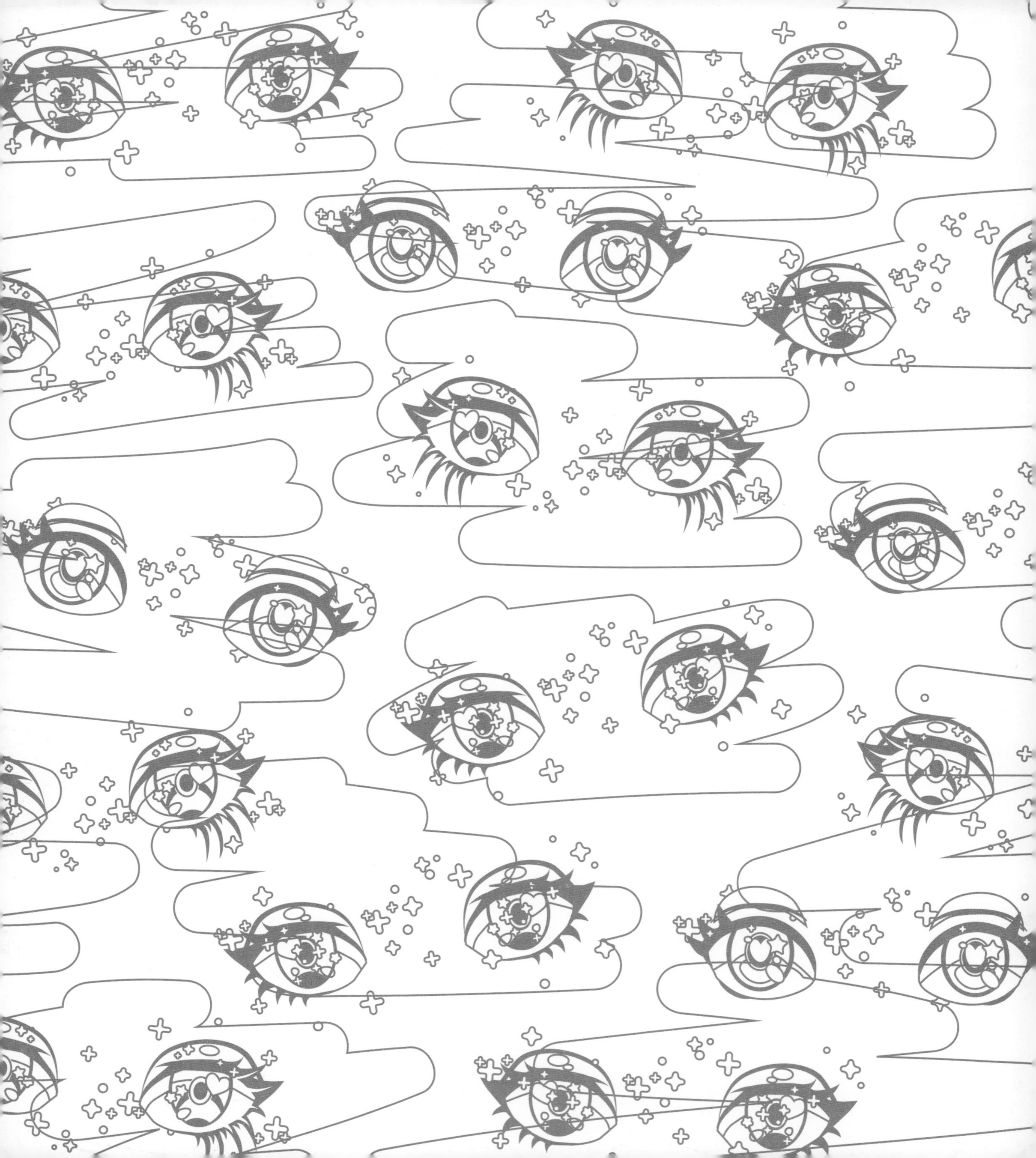

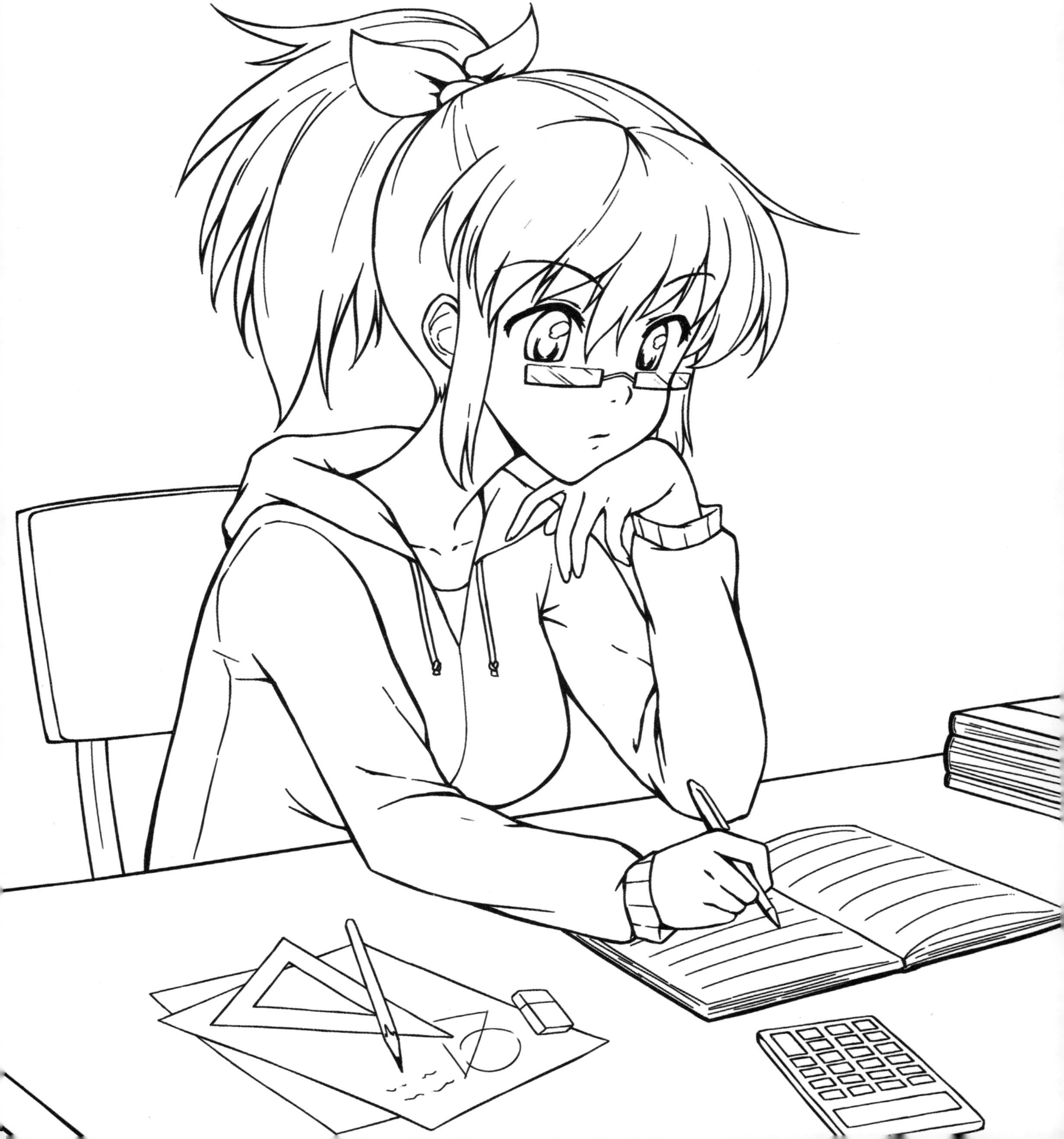

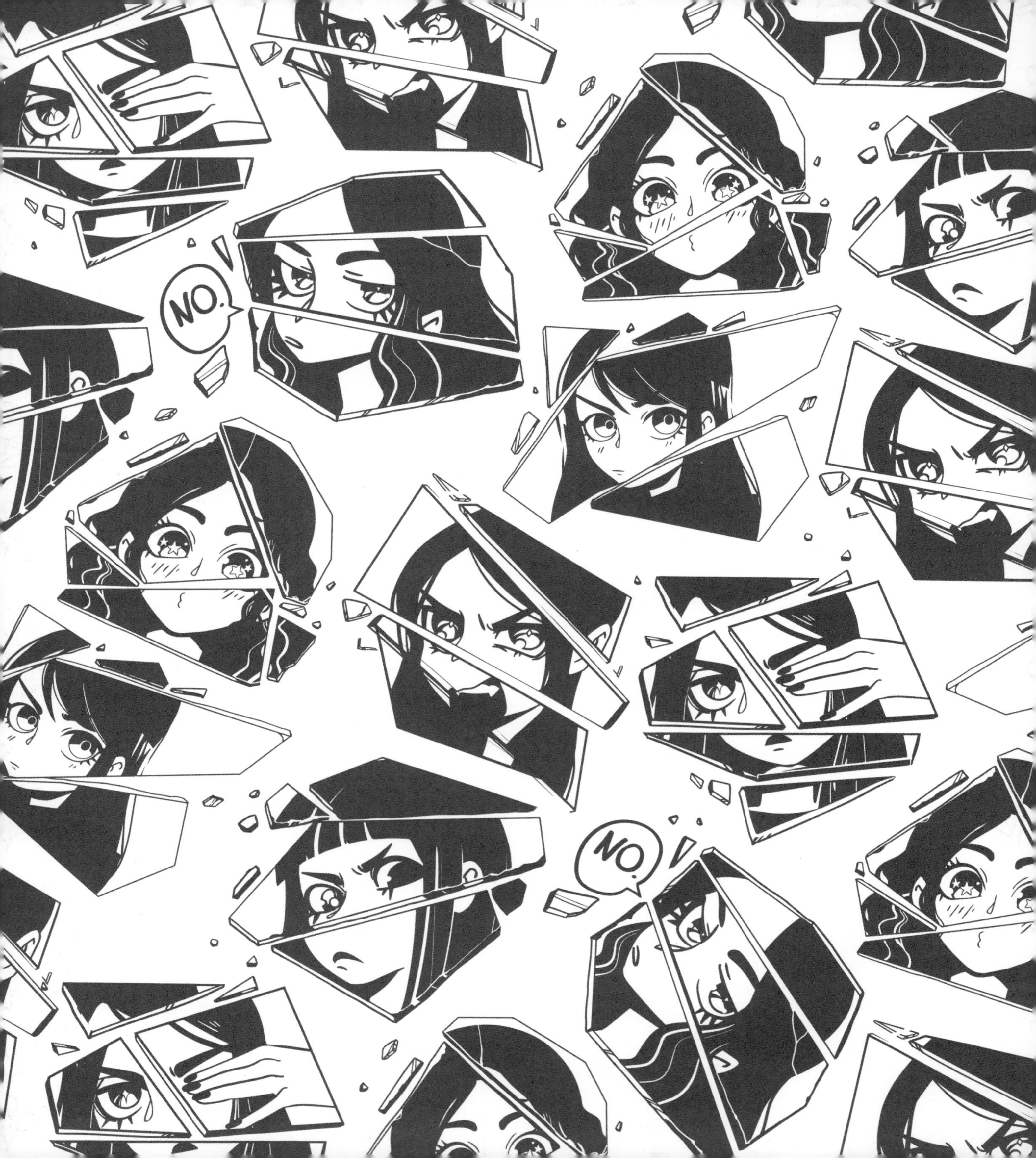
NO.
NO.

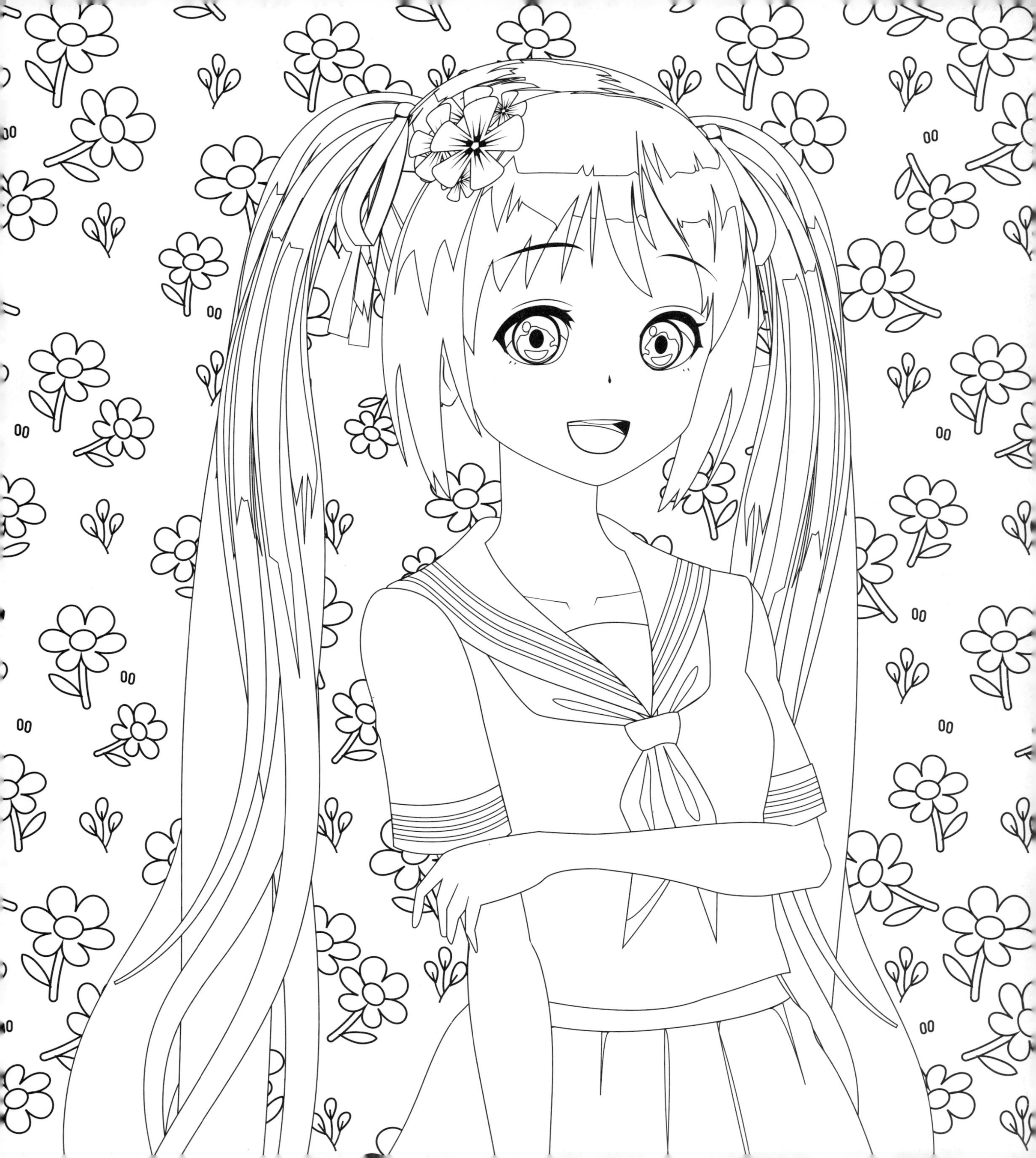

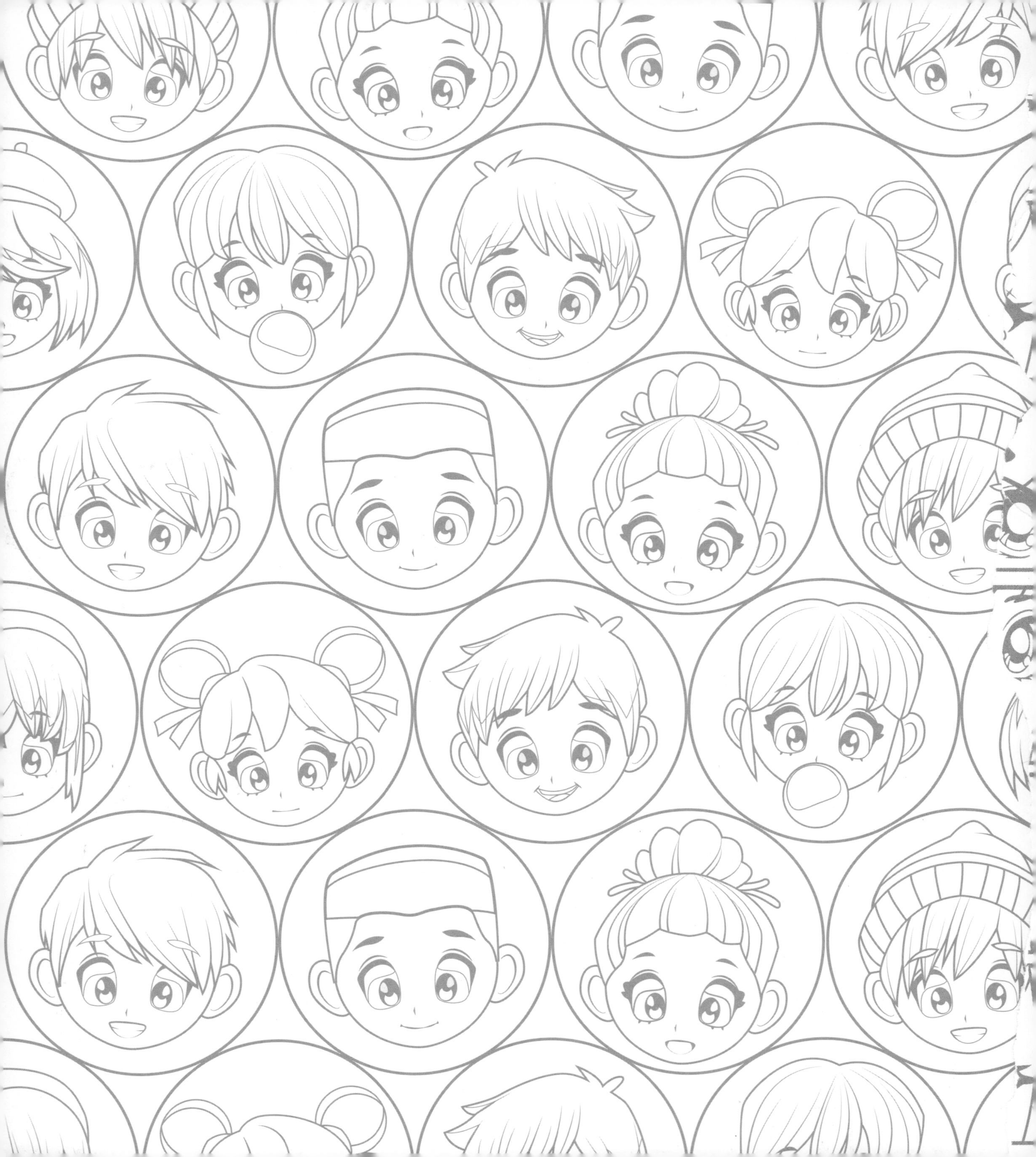

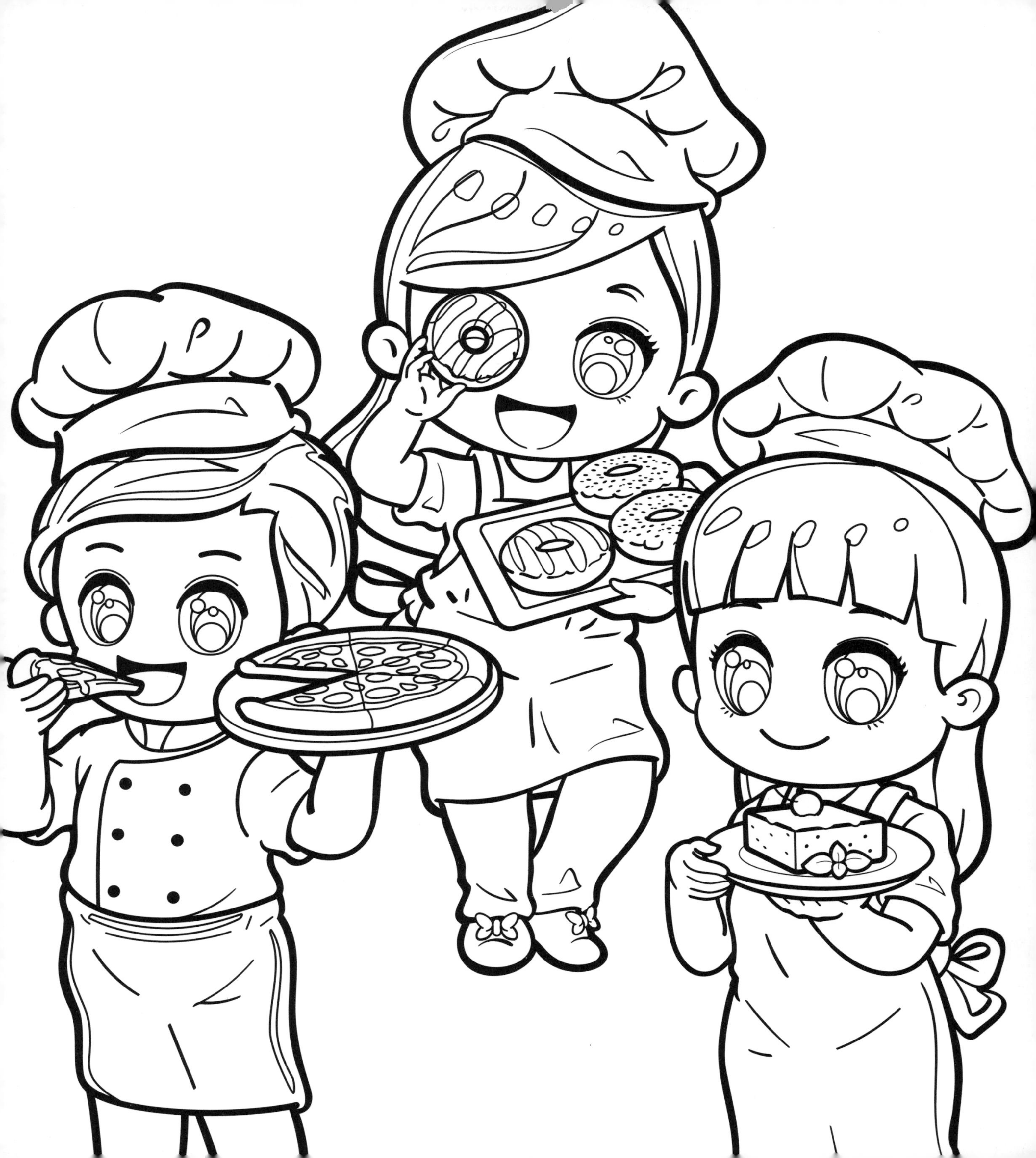

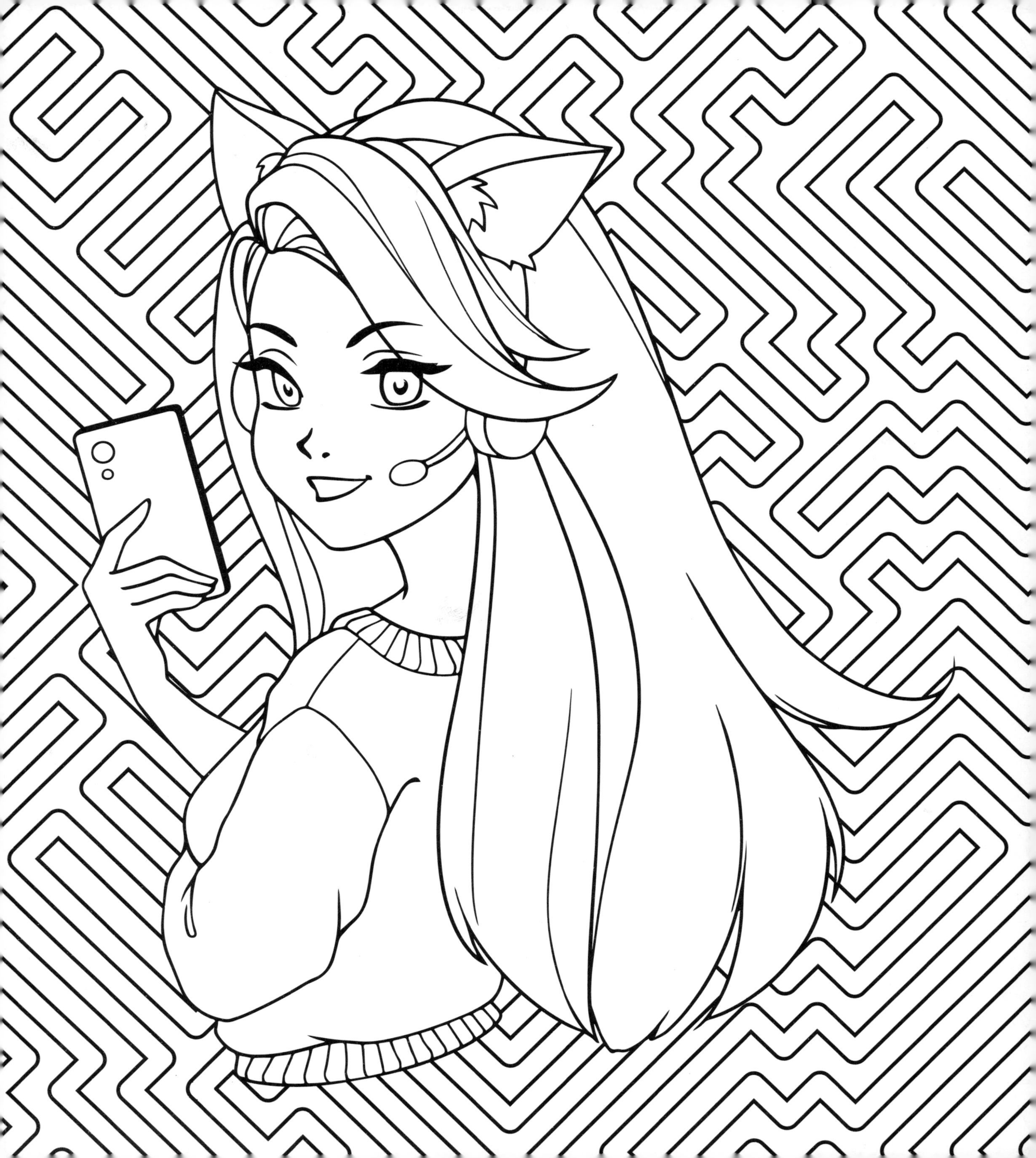

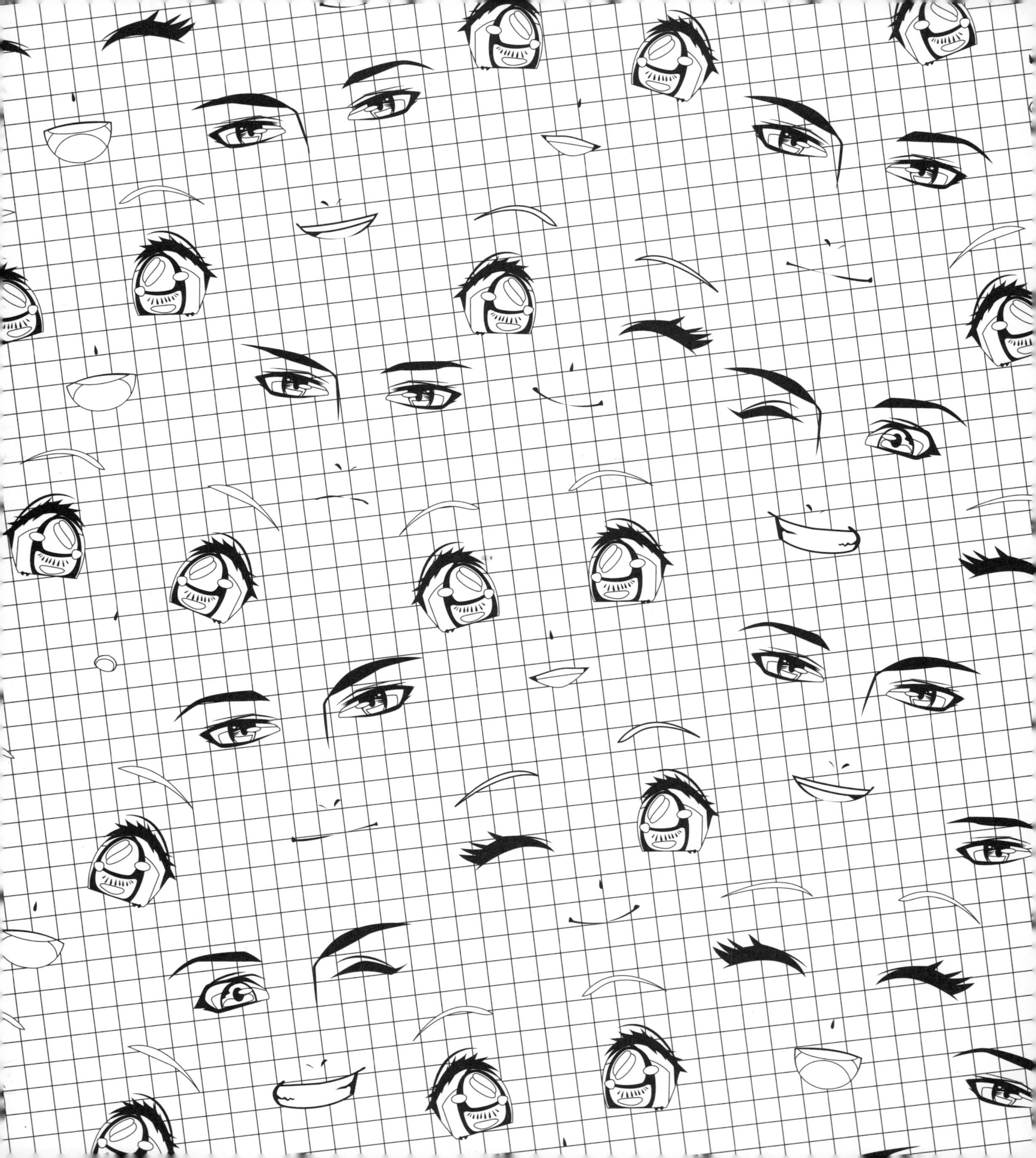

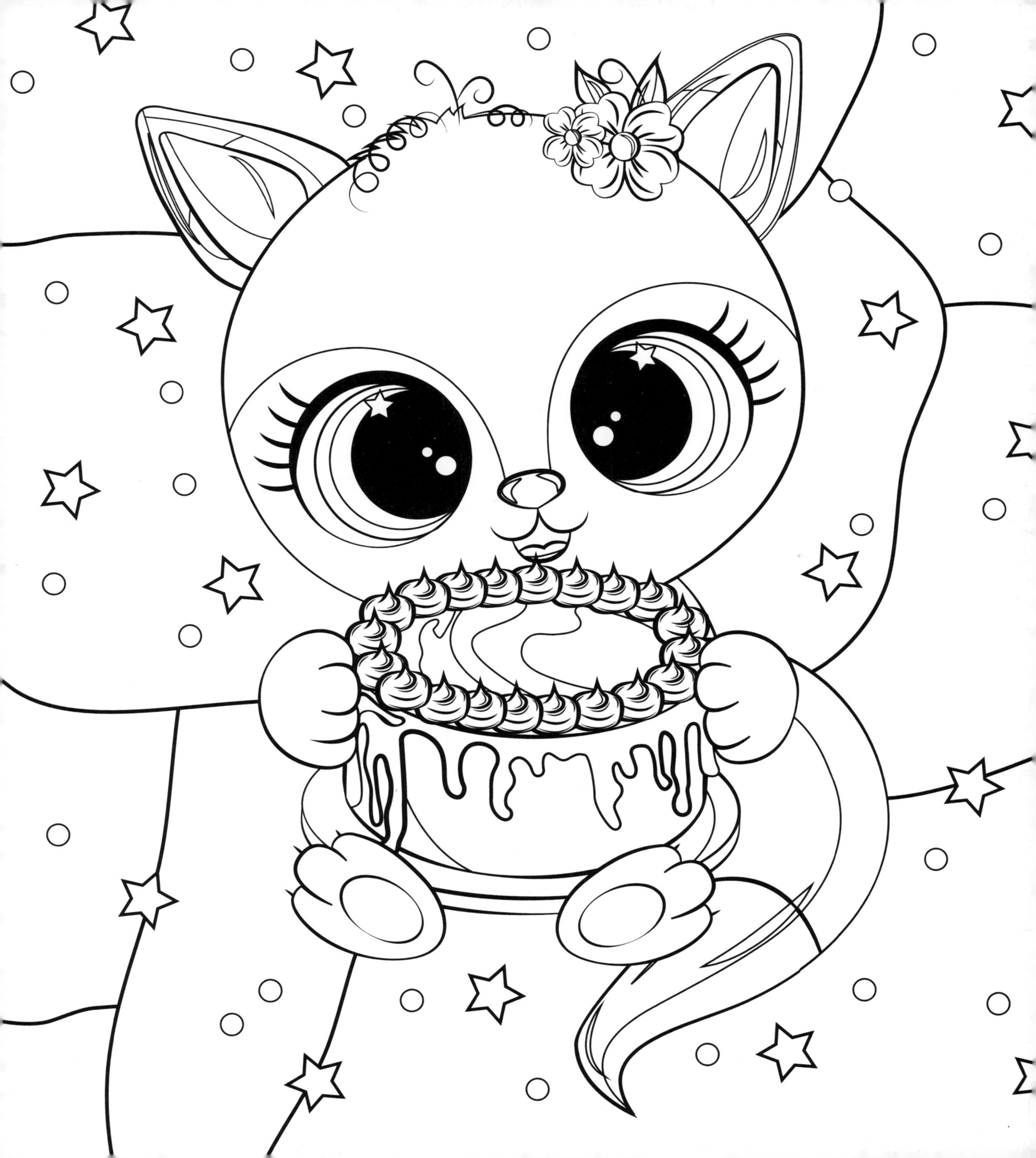

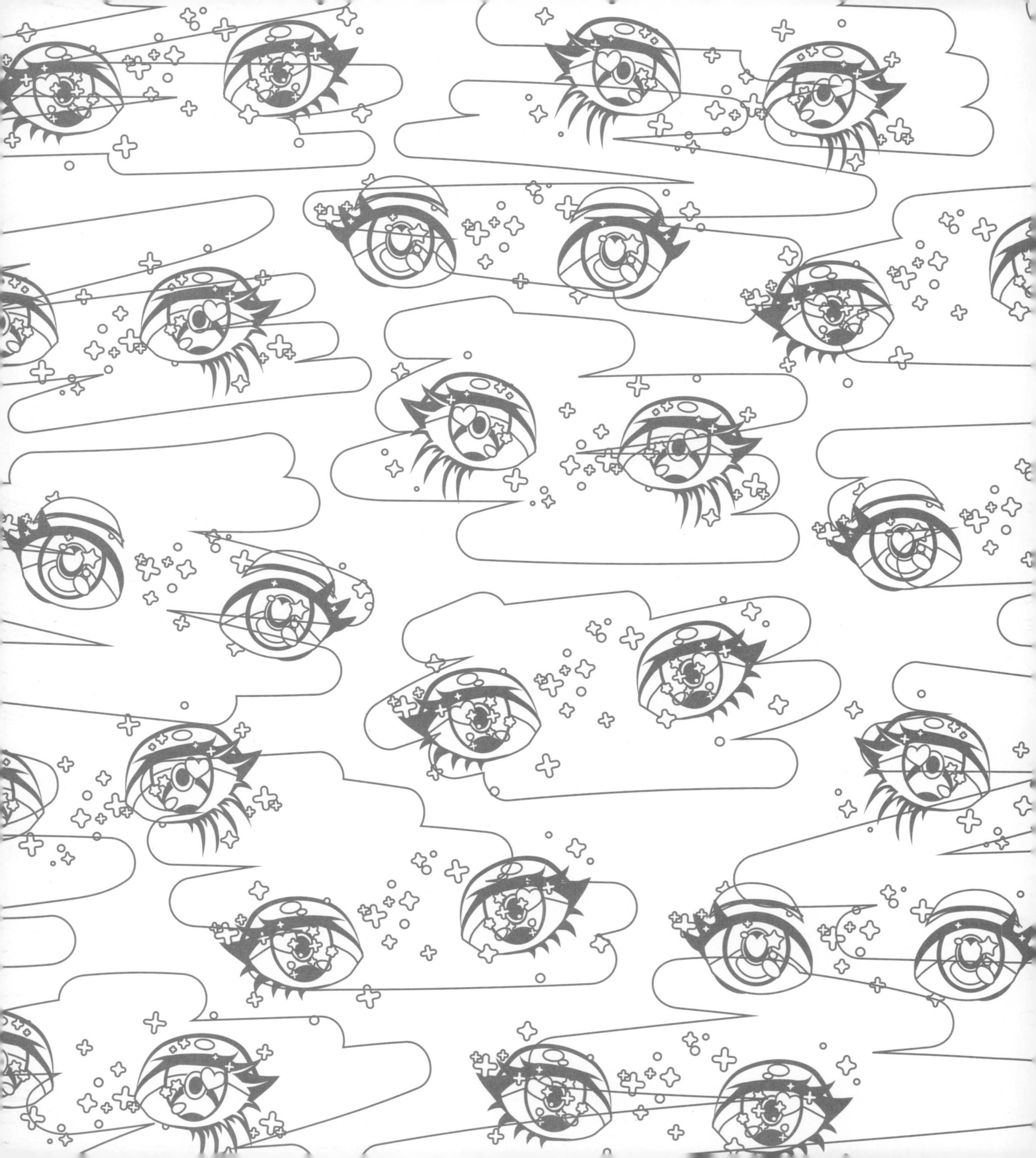

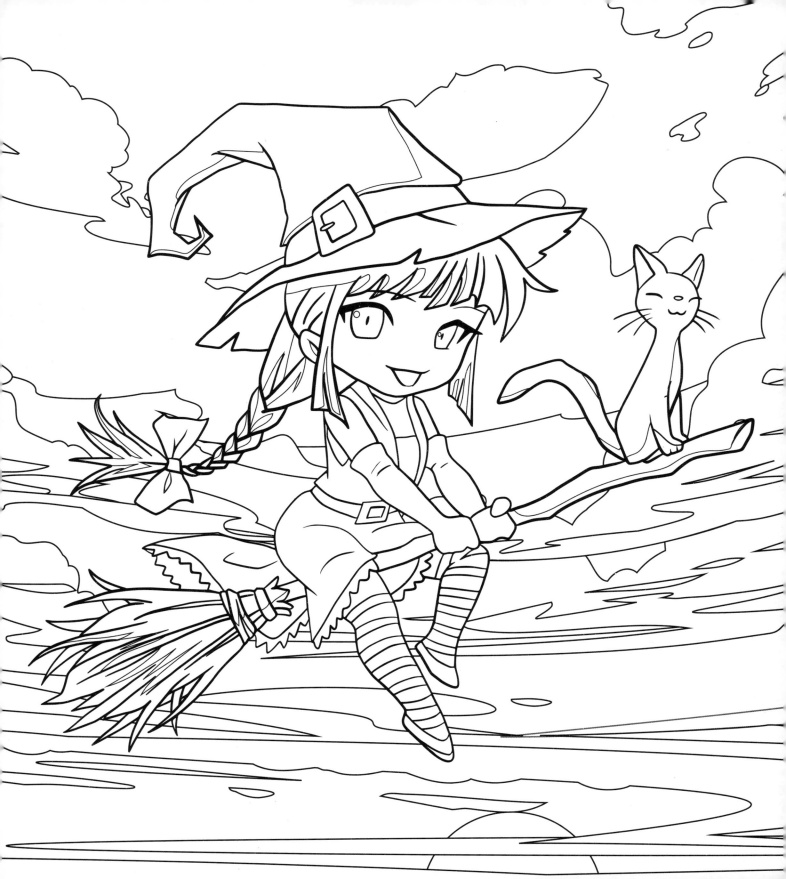

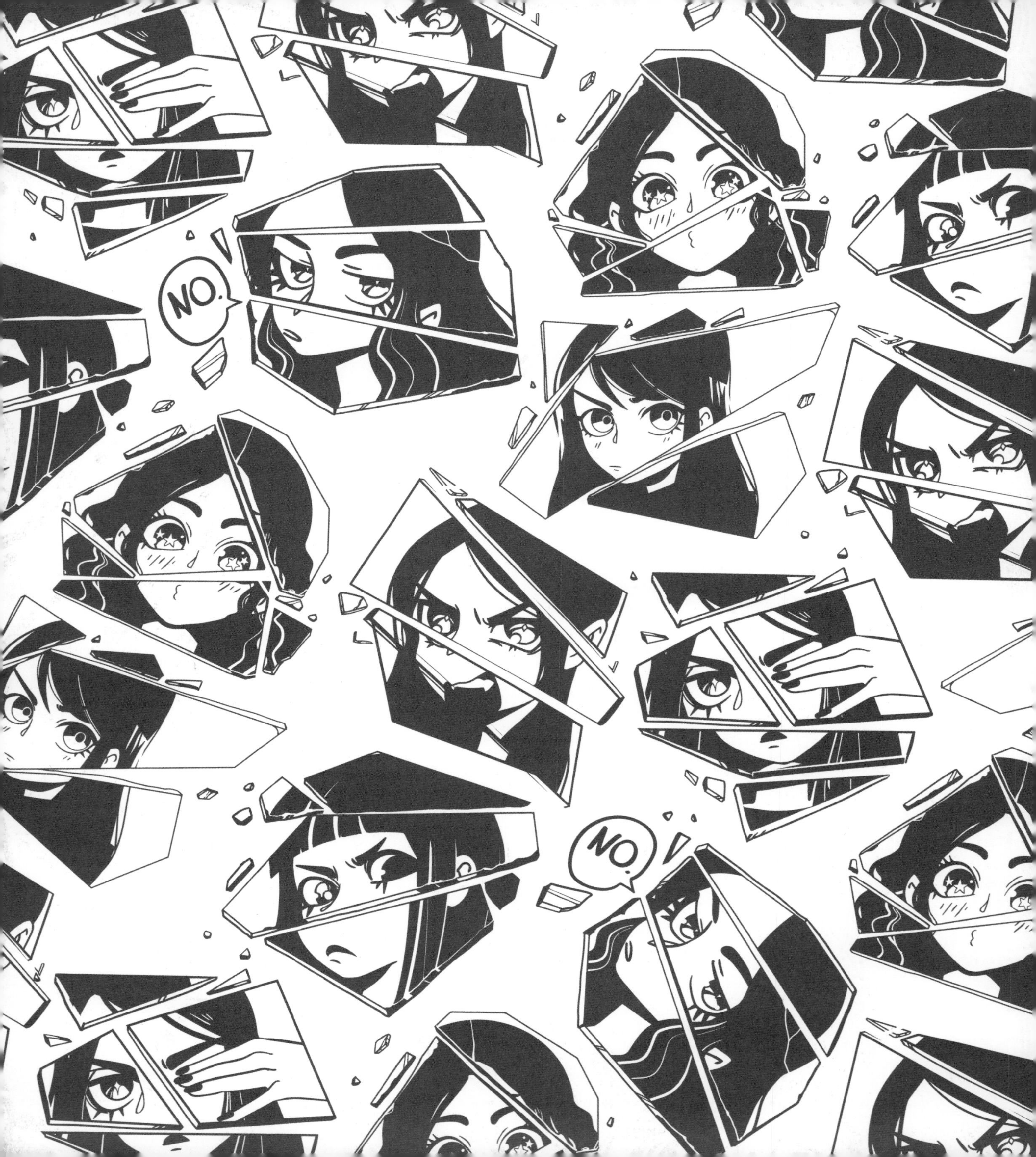
NO.
NO.

Brimming with creative inspiration, how-to projects, and useful information to enrich your everyday life, quarto.com is a favorite destination for those pursuing their interests and passions.

© 2022 Quarto Publishing Group USA Inc.

This edition published in 2022 by Chartwell Books,
an imprint of The Quarto Group
142 West 36th Street, 4th Floor
New York, NY 10018 USA
T (212) 779-4972 F (212) 779-6058
www.Quarto.com

All rights reserved. No part of this book may be reproduced in any form without written permission of the copyright owners. All images in this book have been reproduced with the knowledge and prior consent of the artists concerned, and no responsibility is accepted by producer, publisher, or printer for any infringement of copyright or otherwise, arising from the contents of this publication. Every effort has been made to ensure that credits accurately comply with information supplied. We apologize for any inaccuracies that may have occurred and will resolve inaccurate or missing information in a subsequent reprinting of the book.

10 9 8 7 6 5 4 3 2 1

Chartwell titles are also available at discount for retail, wholesale, promotional, and bulk purchase. For details, contact the Special Sales Manager by email at specialsales@quarto.com or by mail at The Quarto Group, Attn: Special Sales Manager, 100 Cummings Center Suite 265D, Beverly, MA 01915, USA.

ISBN: 978-0-7858-4086-2

Publisher: Wendy Friedman
Editorial Director: Betina Cochran
Creative Director: Pauline Molinari
Editor: Cathy Davis
Designer: Kate Sinclair

All stock design elements © Shutterstock

Printed in China